European Confederation of Institutes
of Internal Auditing (ECIIA) (Ed.)

Global Management Challenges for Internal Auditors

ECIIA Yearbook of Internal Audit 2010/11

Edition under special guidance of Dr. Hans Joachim Büsselberg

With contributions by

Neil Baker, Philipp Friebe, Adrián Garrido, Prof. Dr. Fikret Hadžić, Andreas Herzig, Shqiponja Isufi, Dr. Andreas Langer, Thomas Lohre, Sergey Martynov, Daniel Nelson, Inta Ozolina, Prof. Dr. Burkhard Pedell, Prof. T. Flemming Ruud, Dr. Heinrich Schmelter, Daniela Schmitz, Dr. Hannes Schuh, Amir Softić

ERICH SCHMIDT VERLAG

Bibliographic information published by Die Deutsche Nationalbibliothek
Die Deutsche Nationalbibliothek lists this publication in the Deutsche Nationalbibliografie;
detailed bibliographic data are available in the Internet at http://dnb.ddb.de.

For further information concerning this title please follow this link:
ESV.info/978 3 503 12940 9

ECIIA ivzw
European Confederation of Institutes of Internal Auditing ivzw
Koningsstraat 109–111 bus 5 · 1000 Brussels · Belgium
Tel +32 2 217 33 20 · Fax + 32 2 217 33 20 · http://www.eciia.org

ISBN 978 3 503 12940 9

This paper fulfills the requirements of the
Frankfurter Forderungen of Die Deutsche Nationalbibliothek
and the Gesellschaft für das Buch concerning the paper permanence
and meets the tight regulations of American National Standard
Ansi/Niso Z 39.48-1992 as well as ISO 9706

Printing and Binding: Danuvia Druckhaus, Neuburg

Foreword

Welcome to this our second ECIIA yearbook, which we hope you will find as valuable as the first.

When we produced the ECIIA yearbook last year, we noted that the world had faced a period of economic and financial turmoil. As we face the second half of 2010 and into 2011, stability still seems far away. Governments across the EU have taken measures to halt or slow the financial crisis, but still more is needed. In many countries, including the UK and Greece, people are facing severe cuts to public spending in order to address budget deficits. This may affect many internal audit departments as they too may face cuts in staffing and budgets. This will add another dimension to internal audit work – the need to do more with less. The ability to work smarter will increase in importance over the coming year, and sharing information and knowledge between internal audit teams will be crucial. **Progress through sharing** is the global motto our profession is dedicated to, and sharing the knowledge we have in Europe continues to be a high priority. We are working toward this partly through the publication of our yearbooks, but also through the information that we provide on our website (www.eciia.eu) which was relaunched this year.

This pressure on budgets within internal audit teams does not mean that internal audit has decreased in importance. We wrote last year how corporate governance and risk management is high on the global political agenda. This has not changed, indeed the focus has increased, with many countries producing discussion papers and changes to legislation to improve corporate governance. We have also seen this in the EU, most recently in June 2010 when the Commission launched a public consultation on how to improve corporate governance in financial institutions. Internal Audit has a key role to play, and our advocacy work aims to build relationships with organisations and stakeholders that affect the profession globally.

In this edition you will find articles from around the EU covering the IIA Standards, Corporate Governance, Internal Audit Practices and the future of Internal Audit. We hope that you find them of value.

We would like to thank all the authors and other contributors to this project. We would also like to thank the international project team for making the publication of this yearbook possible: Nicole Schneider-Brennecke, IIA Germany (project lead),

Dr. Matthias Kopetzky, IIA Austria, Nicola Rimmer, IIA – UK and Ireland and Amanda Zute, IIA Latvia. We also would like to thank Marc Slowig of IIA Germany for the support provided. The ECIIA Yearbook Taskforce was led by Dr. Hans Joachim Büsselberg, IIA Germany.

The ECIIA Management Board

Claude Cargou, France
(President)
CEO of Governis, Member of the
Board of IFACI, Chairman of
AXA Spain audit Committee

Phil Tarling, UK & Ireland
(Vice-President)
International Partner, RSM
Bentley Jennison

Dr. Hans Joachim Büsselberg,
Germany
(Project Lead)
Chief Audit Executive AXA
Germany

Carolyn Dittmeier, Director
of Internal Audit of Poste Italiane
Spa

Joanna Mrowicka, Poland
Chief Audit Executive, Poznan
University of Technology

Ali Sir Yardim, Turkey
CIA, CFE, Chief Auditor,
Istanbul Stock Exchange

Tzvetan Tzvetkov, Bulgaria
Head of the Internal Audit,
Bulgarian National Audit Office

Christian Van Nedervelde, Lux-
embourg
Vice President Internal Audit,
SES Group

Pascale Vandenbussche, (Secre-
tary of the Board)
Chief Staff Officer IIA Belgium

The ECIIA

The ECIIA (European Confederation of Institutes of Internal Auditing) represents the beacon of the Internal Audit profession in the wider geographic area of Europe and the Mediterranean basin.

ECIIA exists to promote professional internal auditing – its benefits, competencies, standards and qualifications – to all institutions, bodies, committees and people of influence within its member countries. It undertakes research on topics relating to internal audit, business control, risk management and corporate governance. It publishes position papers, briefings reports and a quarterly newsletter.

Project Team

Dr. Hans Joachim Büsselberg (Head of Task Force), Chief Audit Executive of AXA Konzern AG, Member of the Board of Management IIA Germany, Member of the Board of Management ECIIA (Cologne, Germany)

Nicole Schneider-Brennecke (Project lead), Press and Media Relations Manager, IIA Germany, (Frankfurt, Germany)

Dr. Matthias Kopetzky, CEO, Business Valuation GmbH, Member of the Board of IIA Austria (Vienna, Austria)

Nicola Rimmer, Internal Audit Practitioner and Council Member IIA UK and Ireland (London, United Kingdom)

Amanda Zute, IIA Latvia (Riga, Latvia)

Table of Content

INTERNAL AUDIT PRACTICES

FUTURE OF INTERNAL AUDITING

Internal Audit Standards & Professional Practice Framework

Internal Audit Standards: Everything for Everybody?

By Inta Ozolina, Internal auditor (ACCA, CIA)
The applicability and scope of IAI Standards has been an object of discussion for some time now. One of the issues of these discussions is – whether all companies should apply the Standards to the same extent. Namely, whether smaller companies with smaller size internal audit teams should comply with the same scope of Standards and how they should do it.

We all know that the Standards are extensive, cover most key areas of internal audit profession and work. Even more – the Practice Advisories provide further interpretation of the general statements of the Standards. Of course, the mentioned documents are only for guidance purposes. However, if internal auditors want to bring their work up to the highest quality and recognition, most of them want to be compliant with the Standards and use the phrase 'in compliance with the IAI Standards' in their reports. To be able to do that, a regular external assessment must be done at least once in five years.

And this is where the smaller internal audit teams may face serious challenges or even struggle.

There are companies where audit teams are significant in size, fully equipped with all the necessary specialists to cover all areas of company business; even more so – many bigger teams are divided in compliance and operational auditors. But there are even more companies where internal audit teams are very small in size. The smaller teams can only theoretically be specialized in all the necessary areas. Does that make the team less professional, useful and adding no value to the management and owners? I do not think so. Does it make the compliance for smaller audit teams very hard if not impossible to obtain? Yes, it does...

Even more so, in many companies the management and owners do not appreciate and simply cannot afford huge internal audit teams; the financial crisis has also hit many companies all over the world. Also, in many cases of smaller companies and audit teams respectively, the review of overall control environment is split between internal and external auditors to ensure as much value added to the company management and owners as possible.

Another area where formal compliance with the Standards may be difficult to obtain is documentation. Many business internal auditors try to reduce the amounts of working papers to improve efficiency and effectiveness; often the IA managers (and CAE's) get their hands dirty during audit engagements and the management layers are very limited in small audit teams, thus making the compliance with the formal review requirements very hard to ensure.

The discussion on issues of small audit teams could go on and on. However, the aim of this article is not to diminish the value of Standards as such, just the opposite. Our aim is to increase the quality and reputation of internal audit profession as much as possible. And attestation against Standards is one of the means. However, if small audit teams, irrespective of how professional, qualified and experienced they are, avoid such assessment because the requirements are just unrealistic, the Standards really lose their meaning.

I think it is a high time to raise this discussion and initiate modification of Standards for smaller companies to motivate and promote the quality of work of all internal auditors irrespective on the size of their company and audit team.

International Professional Practices Framework – Overview of the current guidance of the Institute of Internal Auditors

By T. Flemming Ruud, Philipp Friebe, Daniela Schmitz, Shqiponja Isufi

The Institute of Internal Auditors (IIA) has updated the International Professional Practices Framework which came into effect on January 1, 2009. Although the new framework is consistent with the previous framework, it contains some significant changes which are identified and explained in this article.[1]

1   Introduction

Around ten years ago the *Institute of Internal Auditors (IIA)* recognized the need to align the *Professional Practices Framework (PPF)* of Internal Auditing. In the meantime the Internal Audit has gained in importance due to different legislative and regulatory initiatives aimed at improving the Governance, Risk Management and Internal Control of an organization. The PPF has established itself as the structural basis for the activities of the Internal Audit. It is a self-contained framework which is recognized internationally by various regulatory authorities.[2] For example, in Switzerland the *Swiss Financial Market Supervisory Authority (FINMA)* refers to the guidance of the IIA.[3] As a consequence, the Internal Audit profession faced higher expectations and new challenges, which increased the need for rules and guidelines for Internal Auditing. The IIA met these needs by changing the PPF and creating additional requirements, however, the development and mandatory nature of these were not always understood.[4]

With this background the IIA created a task force in 2006 to revise the scope and structure of the PPF and the process for developing and reviewing the individual elements of the framework. The aim of this review was to create more clarity as to the mandatory nature of the elements, to improve transparency in relation to the development of the

---

[1]   Originally published in German, available on http: www.treuhaender.ch.

[2]   Cf. The IIA's Vision for the Future Task Force (2007), p. 3, Bantleon/Unmuth (2008), p. 106 and Baker (2009), p. 56.

[3]   Cf. FINMA-Circular 2008/24 *Supervision and Internal Control banks* (former Circular 06/6 *Supervision and Internal Control* of the Swiss Federal Banking Commission).

[4]   Cf. The IIA's Vision for the Future Task Force (2007), p. 3 and Baker (2009), p. 54.

elements, and to ensure the elements are updated quickly in a predefined development and review process. The framework proposed by the task force was approved by the IIA in summer 2007. In order to emphasize the international focus of the framework, it was renamed as the *International Professional Practices Framework (IPPF)*. The process was completed and became effective in January 2009.[5] At first sight the changes appear to be of rather subordinate character, however the IPPF contains some important changes which are explained in this article. First, the individual elements of the framework are described, then, the important changes to the Standards are introduced and finally, the conclusion evaluates the changed framework and gives an outlook for the future development of the IPPF.

2 Elements of the Updated Framework

The IPPF consists of six elements which are either mandatory or strongly recommended. The updated framework knows two categories, while the previous contained three. The Development and Practice Aids endorsed or developed by the IIA were not suitable for the new concept and were removed.[6] Meanwhile Position Papers and Practice Guides were added to the framework. Figure 1 shows the elements of the previous PPF and the new IPPF.[7]

	IPPF			Removed
Elements	Mandatory	Strongly recommended	Endorsed or developed by the IIA
Former elements — Definition	X		
Code of Ethics	X		
Standards	X		
Practice Advisories		X	
Added — Position Papers		X	
Practice Guides		X	
Removed — Development and Practice Aids			X

Figure 1: Elements of the PPF and the IPPF

---

[5] Cf. The IIA (2009a), p. iii.

[6] Cf. The IIA's Vision for the Future Task Force (2007), p. 2.

[7] All of the elements of the IPPF are available to members of the IIA on http://www.theiia.org. Non-members have access to the Definition of Internal Auditing, the Code of Ethics, the Standards and the Position Papers on this homepage.

18

2.1 Mandatory Elements

As figure 1 shows, the Definition of Internal Auditing, the Code of Ethics and the Standards represent the mandatory elements of the IPPF. "Mandatory" means that all of the members of the IIA must comply with these elements. This also applies to those holding IIA's professional qualifications (e.g. *Certified Internal Auditors – CIA®*) and candidates for such exams.[8]

The Definition of Internal Auditing (cf. Figure 2) describes its underlying purpose, characteristics and scope. Unlike the other elements of the IPPF, the Definition of Internal Auditing was adopted without any changes; its importance and focus were confirmed.

> Internal Auditing is an independent, objective assurance and consulting activity designed to add value and improve an organization's operations. It helps an organization accomplish its objectives by bringing a systematic, disciplined approach to evaluate and improve the effectiveness of Risk Management, Control, and Governance processes.

Figure 2: Definition of Internal Auditing

The Code of Ethics describes the principles for and the expectations relating to the behaviour of individuals and organizations which perform audit engagements. In order to effectively help the board and the management, it is necessary that the Internal Auditors behave in a professional manner. Professionalism provides the basis for trust in the work of the Internal Audit and is distinguished in particular by a high degree of integrity, objectivity, confidentiality and competency. These four principles of the Code of Ethics are supplemented by twelve rules of conduct which must be complied with in order to follow the principles. Apart from a change to the wording, the Code of Ethics was also adopted unchanged.

The Standards are regulations which are principle-based and provide mandatory guides for the performance of Internal Audit activities and represent the core of the IPPF. Three types of Standards are used; Attribute Standards, Performance Standards and Implementation Standards (cf. Figure 3). The Attribute Standards outline the characteristics of individuals and organizations which perform Internal Audit activities. The Performance Standards specify the purpose and procedures of the Internal Audit. They also contain quality criteria, based upon which the services of the Internal Audit can be assessed. The Attribute Standards and the Performance Standards apply to all Internal Audit services. They are supplemented by the Implementation Standards, which contain specific guidelines and are aimed either at

---

[8]   Cf. The IIA (2009a), p. iii.

Assurance (identified by an A, e.g. 2120.A2) or Consulting Services (identified by a C, e.g. 2120.C3). The Standards also include a Glossary which defines the terms and expressions used.

2.2   Strongly Recommended Elements

The strongly recommended elements of the IPPF include the Practice Advisories, Position Papers and Practice Guides (cf. Figure 3). "Strongly recommended" means that the IIA advocates compliance with these elements and asks Internal Auditors to be guided by these regulations.[9]

The Practice Advisories provide Internal Auditors with guidance concerning the implementation of the Code of Ethics and the Standards by specifying approaches, methods and best practice. The guidance refers to global, national and sector-specific aspects, to specific audit engagements and to legislative and regulatory matters. In the review of the framework, the content of the Practice Advisories was changed and their scope reduced. The previous content of the Practice Advisories is now partly included in the Practice Guides and in the interpretations which supplement the Standards.[10]

The Position Papers help interested parties, including individuals who do not work in Internal Audit, to understand the essential aspects of Governance, Risk Management and Internal Control. The Position Papers primarily explain the roles of Internal Audit in relation to these processes. For example, the Position Paper "The Role of Internal Auditing in Enterprise-Wide Risk Management" describes the role of Internal Audit within the scope of Risk Management.[11] Included in the IPPF, the previous existing Position Papers have gained in importance.

The Practice Guides are detailed guidelines concerning the performance of Internal Audit activities. They include specific processes and procedures, examples are Practice Guides relating to IT audits and other IT-related issues.

---

[9]   Cf. The IIA (2009a), p. iii.

[10]   Cf. The IIA (2009a), p. v.

[11]   Cf. Ruud/Sommer (2006) and The IIA (2009b).

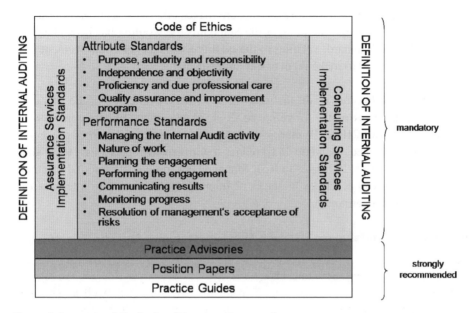

Figure 3: International Professional Practices Framework

3 Important Changes to the Standards

The Standards shown above represent the core of the IPPF. In the revision of the framework the Standards were updated, but their original meaning was not changed. In the following the important changes will be revealed.

3.1 Interpretations

The Standards are newly supplemented by interpretations which explain the key terms and the content of the Standards. In total 19 interpretations were added which are shown directly after the relevant Standard. In order to fully comply with the Standards, the interpretations must also be considered.[12]

3.2 Existing Standards Adjusted

In order to emphasize the mandatory nature of the Standards, in most of the Standards the word "should" was replaced by the word "must". "Must" specifies an unconditional requirement.

However, in five Standards (1010, 2050, 2130.A2, 2130.A3, 2220.A2) the word "should" is still used. In these cases compliance with the Standards is expected,

---

12 Cf. The IIA (2009a), p. 12.

unless the application of due professional care makes otherwise seem appropriate in the given circumstances.[13] In some of the Standards the wording has been changed. For example, the Standards relating to the quality assurance and improvement program were rephrased to make them easier understandable.

The scope of the Internal Audit includes the systematic evaluation of the adequacy and the effectiveness of the Governance, Risk Management and Internal Control processes (Standard 2100). To clarify the interrelationship of these three processes, the order was changed. Standard 2110 relates to Governance (previously Risk Management). Standard 2120 relates to Risk Management (previously Internal Control), while Standard 2130 describes the tasks of Internal Audit relating to Internal Control (previously Governance).

Five terms were added to the Standards Glossary (cf. Figure 4).[14]

Information Technology Controls
Controls that support business management and governance as well as provide general and technical controls over information technology infrastructures such as applications, information, infrastructure, and people.

Information Technology Governance
Consists of the leadership, organizational structures, and processes that ensure that the enterprise's information technology sustains and supports the organization's strategies and objectives.

Risk Appetite
The level of risk that an organization is willing to accept.

Technology based Audit Techniques
Any automated audit tool, such as generalized audit software, test data generators, computerized audit programs, specialized audit utilities, and computer-assisted audit techniques (CAATs).

Significance
The relative importance of a matter within the context in which it is being considered, including quantitative and qualitative factors, such as magnitude, nature, effect, relevance, and impact. Professional judgment assists Internal Auditors when evaluating the significance of matters within the context of the relevant objectives.

Figure 4: New terms in the IIA Glossary

---

[13]   Cf. Hahn (2009), p. 35.

[14]   Cf. Bantleon/Unmuth (2008), p. 107.

3.3 New Standards

In addition to the changes to the existing Standards, six new Standards were issued. Standard 1010 states that the mandatory nature of the Definition of Internal Auditing, the Code of Ethics and the Standards must be recognized in the Internal Audit charter. Moreover, the Chief Audit Executive should discuss the Definition of Internal Auditing, the Code of Ethics and the Standards with the senior management and the board. Standard 1111 demands that the Chief Audit Executive communicates and interacts directly with the board. The IIA stresses the importance of the Chief Audit Executive having direct access to the board or the audit committee for reasons of independence. Standard 2110.A2 specifies that the Internal Audit activity must assess whether the IT Governance of the organization supports the strategies and objectives of the organization. According to Standard 2120.A2, when evaluating the Risk Management processes the Internal Audit activity must take into account the potential for the occurrence of fraud and how the organization manages fraud risks. Furthermore, Standard 2120.C3 now specifies that when assisting senior management or line management in establishing or improving Risk Management processes, Internal Auditors must refrain from assuming any management responsibility by actually managing risks. The Internal Audit activity supports the managers of an organization by evaluating the adequacy and effectiveness of the Risk Management processes, proposing any improvements and providing certain advisory activities.[15] In doing so, Internal Audit can make the managers aware of risks; however, the management of risks is not the responsibility of Internal Audit. The roles of Internal Audit within the scope of Risk Management are therefore specified in more detail in the above-mentioned Position Paper. Finally, the new Standard 2430 makes it clear that Internal Auditors may report that their engagements are conducted in conformance with the Standards only if the results of the quality assurance and improvement program support this statement.[16]

4   Process Improvements

In reviewing the framework, the IIA has also changed the development and review processes of the individual elements. The IPPF now only includes elements which have been developed and passed in clearly structured and transparent processes. These processes make it possible for the IIA to issue guidelines faster. They also provide Internal Auditors with the opportunity to have a greater influence on the development of and the changes to the elements of the IPPF by contributing ideas and suggestions for improvement.[17]

---

[15]   Cf. Ruud/Sommer (2006), p. 253.
[16]   Cf. Standard 1300.
[17]   Cf. The IIA (2009a), p. iii and Baker (2009), p. 57-59.

The IIA decided that there will be a complete review of the appropriateness of the IPPF every three years. The existing guidelines can therefore be updated if they are no longer appropriate.[18]

5   Conclusion

With the updated IPPF the IIA has acted to the changes in the environment of the Internal Audit profession. The IPPF clarifies the increased professionalization of the Internal Audit and, compared to the previous framework, provides more clarity concerning the mandatory nature of the individual elements. Furthermore, the new interpretations and the narrowed Practice Advisories contribute to better understanding of the Standards. However, it remains to be seen how the IPPF will stand the test in practice.

Due to the new development and review processes, the IIA is able to adapt the elements of the IPPF quicker. For example, new Practice Advisories and Practice Guides were issued in 2009 and 2010. Internal Auditors get the opportunity to influence the further development of the IPPF thanks to the new development and review processes. Internal Auditors are encouraged to contribute with ideas and suggestions for continued improvement for the IPPF.

References

Baker, Neil (2009): A renewed framework, in: Internal Auditor, February 2009, Vol. 66, Issue 1, p. 54-59.

Bantleon, Ulrich/Unmuth, Anja (2008): "Das Internationale Regelwerk der Beruflichen Praxis des Institute of Internal Auditors (IIA)" (The International Professional Practices Framework of the Institute of Internal Auditors (IIA))", in: Zeitschrift Interne Revision, 3/2008, p. 106-109.

Hahn, Ulrich (2009): "Die Internationalen Grundlagen für die berufliche Praxis der Internen Revision 2009" (The international fundamentals for the professional practice of Internal Audit 2009), in: Zeitschrift Interne Revision, 1/2009, p. 34-37.

IIA Austria (2009): "Internationale Standards für die berufliche Praxis der Internen Revision 2009" (International Standards for the Professional Practice of Internal Auditing), Vienna 2009.

Ruud, Flemming/Sommer, Katerina (2006): "Internes Audit und Enterprise Risk Management" (Internal Audit and Enterprise Risk Management), in: Der Schweizer Treuhänder, 4/2006, p. 253-257.

The IIA (2009a): International Professional Practices Framework (IPPF), Altamonte Springs 2009.

The IIA (2009b): The Role of Internal Auditing in Enterprise-Wide Risk Management, Altamonte Springs 2009.

The IIA's Vision for the Future Task Force (2007): Guiding the Internal Audit Profession to Excellence, Altamonte Springs 2007.

---

[18]   Cf. IIA Austria (2009), p. 10.

Corporate Governance & Risk Management

Efficient Risk Management in Leasing Companies

By Prof. Dr. Fikret Hadžić and Amir Softić[19]

1   Introduction

After a decrease of 9.1 % in the leasing market in Bosnia and Herzegovina during the year 2008, in the previous year, 2009, the data was even more unfavourable. As a result of the recession, leasing markets recorded a further decrease of more then 60 %, until the number of signed contracts for the same period decreased by 40 %.[20]

The decrease indicated follows European trends in this area. So in the first half of the year 2009, the leasing market in Europe recorded a decrease of 35.8 % compared with the same period in 2008. The biggest decrease occurred in the countries in which the recession had the most significant effect, i.e. in the countries in which the leasing market has, in previous years, recorded a significant increase. In the period outlined, the most significant decrease has been recorded in the leasing market of Lithuania (81.33 %), Ukraine (77.15 %), Russia (73.13 %), and Estonia (69.24 %). The smallest decrease (around 16 %) has been recorded by leasing markets in Sweden and Holland.[21]

The word *Leasing* can be defined as a written contract between two parties: the leasing company (as lessee) and the beneficiary of the equipment (lease recipient). In this business transaction the lessee acquires the leasing subject (movable or fixed property) and gives it to the lease recipient to use for a certain period of time with the lease recipient being obliged to periodically pay the lessee in accordance with the contract.

Leasing is a very important source of medium and long-term financing. It is an efficient asset for the acquisition of required production and other equipment, as well as the property necessary for performing business activities. It is especially convenient for small and medium-sized businesses that, quite often, do not have an access to commercial bank loans. Also, leasing enables the financing of vehicle acquisition

---

[19]   Dr. Fikret Hadžić is a professor at the University of Economy in Sarajevo (fikret.hadzic@efsa.unsa.ba); Amir Softić, dipl.oec is a member of ASA Finance d.d. management, and is responsible for risk management (amir.softic@asa.ba).

[20]   See www.leasing.org.ba; www.banka.hr; www.poslovni.hr - accessed on 21 March 2010.

[21]   www.leaseurope.org – accessed on 21 March 2010.

for civilian purposes which boosts domestic consumption, and thus creates conditions for more dynamic economic development. Because of its developing function many countries encourage the establishment and work of leasing companies. In developed countries about one quarter of all acquisitions of business equipment is financed through leasing. Estimates also point that today, only in developing countries, the financing value of new equipment and vehicles by means of leasing, amounts to over 40 billion dollars a year.

Financial leasing is the most frequently used type of leasing. With this leasing, during the repayment period, the subject of lease continues to be owned by the lessee. Upon the repayment of the last instalment, ownership of the subject is transferred to the beneficiary. During the lease period, the lease recipient is the only beneficiary who has the exclusive right to use the subject of the leasing.

With operating leasing, the period of its duration is significantly shorter than the usage life of the leased subject. Therefore, after the lease contract expires the equipment is still owned by the lessee and may be leased to a new beneficiary. As outlined, there are other types of leases such as "leasing with lever", leasing with a term adjustment of the rent clause, direct and indirect leasing and others.

However, regardless of the type of leasing, each of them is connected to different types of risks. These risks directly affect the leasing company business, and in that context we can talk about leasing company risks as well. In this paper we will outline some of the most significant risks that leasing companies have been faced with, primarily rental subject risk, and activities and measures of its identification, quantification, control and risk protection.

2   Specifics of Leasing Companies' Risks

Depending on the nature of the lease, the business of leasing companies is related to the variety of risks. Apart from those that are almost all financial, institutions faced with (credit, liquidity risk, concentration, price risk, tax, collection of payments risk, portfolio risks, and a whole set of operating risks), leasing companies, as one of the most significant, specially characterizes leasing i.e. rental subject risk.

Leasing alone, in its structure, carries a high dependability on the basic business of the service user, but also on the secondary market of the leasing subject. Both of these aspects have to be carefully analyzed in the risk assessment process. A decline of interest in certain leasing subjects, significantly increases their approval risks and leads leasing companies to an almost identical dilemma, as it does the banks. The question raised is: how to adjust the financing philosophy by determining the points of the optimal relationship between the value of the leasing subject (*asset-based financing*) and primary credit worthiness generated from the future cash flow of the leasing service applicant.

The dilemma between profitability based on future cash flow (EVA – *Economic Value Added* – approach) and the existence of a secondary market for leasing subject redemption, evidently brings leasing houses closer to the primary function and way of working of commercial banks. In this way they encounter the strong need to develop a comprehensive concept of identification, measurement, management and risk monitoring.

Since 2009 all leasing companies in the Federation of B&H transferred to the supervision system of Agency for Federation of B&H banking. In the first quarter of 2010, the Agency started issuing work permits to leasing houses. The legal framework for the companies in the Federation of B&H (FB&H) represents a law on leasing in the Federation of B&H and decisions by the Agency for banking in the Federation of B&H that regulate the establishment and work of leasing companies in the Federation of B&H.

With this regulated framework there are conditions for establishment, business, cessation of the work of leasing companies, leasing contracts, rights and obligations of the subjects in leasing business, termination of leasing contracts, registration of ownership and other rights over leasing subjects, and areas: risk management, financial reporting and monitoring of leasing companies business.[22]

The adoption of this Law only represents a milestone in the work of leasing companies, which up to now worked under some kind of "semi-illegal conditions". However, regardless of the adoption of this legal framework, it is evident that the global economy crisis influenced the change in the work philosophy and in particular, leasing companies' risk management.

Risk management is currently the most significant aspect of business that affects the change to the complete organisational structure, politics and working procedures of leasing companies. In these companies in particular, we can identify four basic areas of risk management:

– Management of process and decision tools,
– Determination and evaluation of leasing subject value,
– Management of collection process and monitoring of leasing portfolio, and
– Management of reserves for leasing business losses.

---

[22] Law on leasing in the Federation of B&H, *Official Journal of F&iH, no. 85/08,* dated 26 December 2008, and appropriate decision from Agency for **Federation of B&H banking.**

The establishment of adequate standards and their complete implementation in the framework of the outlined segments represents the framework of an efficient risk management system.

3   Management of Process and Decision Tools

The objective of risk management and the forming of reserves is assurance of adequate control and quality assessment of receivables, using certain criteria and tools. In that way, the approval process of leasing services, criteria of credit worthiness and repayment ability assessment, as well as monitoring existing portfolios, needs to assure early identification of problematic receivables and adequate assessment and efficient risk management for minimisation of losses.

In this part of the work, we will represent the possible organization model of the decision process, which assures efficiency, standardisation and risk management control.

The basic process should consist of three phases:

–   Approval of the leasing service,
–   Checking documentation, booking and cession of the leasing subject, and
–   Monitoring of the leasing portfolio.

The complete process of approval, booking and monitoring is not possible to set up exclusively on written procedures, no matter how good they are. Written procedures present only the required but not necessary condition of its implementation. Experience gained by the most developed financial groups showed that for an efficient and adequately control process (which needs to be in service to protect assets and achieve a competitive advantage), it is necessary to develop an IT supported application. We will call this type of application a *"front-end"* system whose primary task is to direct the work processes of all employees, based on the current policies and procedures of leasing companies.

The "front-end" system has a start and end application for recording all data relating to a certain business transaction / leasing service. It includes data about the client, transaction, leasing subject and collateral, leasing application status, scoring result, and repayment of leasing service, collection activities, the efficiency of the process and other important elements. In the system, for the purpose of increasing efficiency and reducing manual work, contract forms and other required documentation that is automatically generated after approval of the leasing service can be integrated.

Also, from the system reports on the leasing application status, efficiency of the approval process by phases, structure of allocated *scoring* zones/ratings, as well as the quality of the repayment service towards: *scoring* zones/ratings, advisers, regions and similar, statistics on collection activities, results of collection, monitoring of *scoring* parameters and others can automatically be generated.

To be functional, the *"front-end"* application needs to, at least, contain:

- An established centralised system for monitoring leasing request processes,
- An established automated counter of days of retention of application with sales staff and risks, with an independent status change application (e.g.: being processed, approved, declined, client withdrew and similar). A change of application status is performed as per determined by a Gantt work process chart,
- Established automated reports on efficiency of process, in total and per processing phase, and per responsible person,
- A developed electronic signature system,
- A developed *scoring* tool for individuals and credit ratings for legal entities. That should be, based on statistic models, a model that is developed including qualitative and quantitative factors, and credit history as well. *Scoring* zone and credit ratings need to be related to the texts that describe the zone, risks, and that determine the holder of the competency and that make reference on approval to the maximal amount of rent/lease, and
- A developed system of competency holders. These can be individual holders or a collective body. It is desirable that the primary holder of the credit competency is a credit board which can delegate competencies to lower levels in accordance with the rulebook on authorisations in the leasing company.

Generally, financial institutions that deal with any kind of crediting need to have an approved rulebook on competencies, in which it is unambiguously regulated to whom the competencies have been allocated, under which conditions and up to which maximum amount. The amount of approved competencies are always related to the estimated level of risk (expected probability of lateness), and to the total exposure to the client and group of related parties. A rulebook on competencies needs to regulate levels of decision-making in cases of recognised higher risk or specific situations (reputation risks, risk of particular industrial branch and similar). Within the delegation of competencies, the principle of *'four eyes"* needs to be established on all levels of decision-making. The rulebook on competencies needs to regulate the set of rules for competency usage and the ways *prohibition and escalation rights* are used.

All delegated competencies need to be monitored with assurance of adequate reports on using competencies and the quality of the approved ranking within individual and collective authorization.

4 Determination and Evaluation of Leasing Subject Value

In this phase we come to the key element, in both risk assessment and portfolio monitoring that includes an evaluation of the real market value of the leasing subject. Actually, the evaluation of the real marketable value of the leasing subject represents a basic security lever of the leasing company. The principle of education and presentation of reserves for losses in leasing business, regulated by authorised regulators, deals with the net principle, within which the base for losses is decreased by the market value of the leasing subject. This is an important step in relation to the regulation of education of reserves in commercial banks, where the gross principle is used regardless of the collateral value.

Bearing this fact in mind, which *de facto* includes International Accounting Standard IAS 39 as well; it is evident how important it is for leasing companies to establish a high quality monitoring system which will include a methodology of internal evaluation of the leasing subject value and a system which regularly updates it.

In addition, regulations by an authorised regulator, that deals with education and maintenance of reserves for losses, predict that leasing companies are obliged to form reserves as per the gross principle (without a decrease of the leasing subject value) if they are not in possession of movable leasing subjects for matured liabilities over 180 days and if they are not in possession of fixed leasing subjects for matured liabilities over 360 days.[23] In this way, the development of an efficient repossession and evaluation system of the leasing subject becomes a key factor of leasing companies' risk management that we will discuss further later in this paper.

Currently leasing companies, to meet the basic standards, are obligated to keep records of each individual leasing subject, with data on their age and the normative rate for value decrease, minimally in accordance with the current decreasing values of movables, used by authorised customs controls in B&H.

By analysing these regulations in part of the evaluation of motor vehicle values, it is evident that they can not be the "right base" for evaluating a leasing subject, as it is primarily based on three basic factors: age of the vehicle, engine size and number of kilometres travelled. We believe that these elements represent the required, but not

---

[23] Decision of Agency for FB&H banking on minimum level and way of forming, managing and maintaining reserves for losses and leasing companies' risk management.

necessary condition for establishing an efficient evaluation system and an adequate methodology for calculating the basis for losses from a leasing business.

Specialist agencies for evaluating vehicles across the world have developed a more detailed and sophisticated system for assessing value. For example the EUROTAX system[24] which is available for our leasing houses includes factors such as: type of vehicles, equipment, geographical area of use and other.

An evaluation of the motor vehicle market value needs to at least include following elements:

- Purchase value of vehicle that includes additional equipment as well,
- Type of vehicle,
- Obsolescence of the vehicle type (innovations on identical models and market updates as additional value),
- Geographical area (quality of transport communications),
- Time depreciation per kilometre travelled,
- General state of the vehicle (technical performance which includes cleanliness and interior state of the vehicle),
- Investments in vehicle repairs,
- Number of previous owners and the way the vehicle is used,
- Previous damage, way and quality of repairs performed on vehicle,
- Supply and demand as a key element, based on forming prices on regional car dealerships.

These entire elements can, by corrective factors (considerations), be calibrated into a unique formula, that by means of a developed IT system can automatically generate the value of a vehicle with the possibility of manual correction by a responsible person or office.

It is evident that the relationship between supply and demand is particularly important in various types of equipment (production line, construction and industrial machines and other), where there is a possibility of a pronounced deviation between the book and market value. The market value with these types of leasing subjects primarily depends on demand elements. In that sense, the market analysis, at primary risk evaluation has a very important role, so we recommend the use of external analysis and evaluations as well, especially for high risk exposures.

---

[24] System for assessing vehicle value: www.eurotaxglass.co.uk.

4.1 Equipment Risks at Leasing

In contrast to the banks and other financial institutions, the main risk that is noticeable in leasing companies that requires special attention is the "equipment risk". Risk of equipment i.e. assets that are the subject of a leasing contract, implies dangers and unwanted financial and material effects that can arise from giving such equipment on a lease. Such risk is reflected in the decrease in the value of that equipment through the duration time of the leasing contract, then through material damage to the equipment when carrying out the business activity by the leasing recipient and other.

"What we can say with certainty is that in most cases the value of the equipment will decrease, but what needs to be determined is how fast and at what value"[25]. A poor evaluation of the outline parameters will have a significant influence on the leasing repayment.

Every lessee expects that a certain number of leasing recipients will not be able to pay their leasing liabilities. These expectations are calculated by rent value and part of these rents is separated as a reserve for potential cases on non-payment. Income from the sale of the equipment that is the subject of the leasing represents the main source of cash assets for recovery when a leasing recipient is no longer able to fulfil their obligations.

If the value of the equipment is less than expected, reserves will not be sufficient and the lessee will suffer the loss. The risk value of the lessee's cash assets varies over time. The variability of that risk depends on (1) rents that have already been paid by the leasing recipient (the more rent that has been paid off, the less cash is exposed to the risk), and (2) the type of leasing – financial leasing or leasing with lever. There are certainly many factors that affect the future value of the equipment, but we will outline only some of them:

- *Physical*– represents all material damage to the equipment that can be noticed during its use and when performing certain activities by the leasing recipient,
- *Technical* – represents factors that can arise during manufacture of improved equipment model,
- *Regulation* – factors that are noticed over time and caused by changes to legal standards relating to the equipment,
- *Demand* – represents demand for the equipment by different sides in order to satisfy its traditional needs (e.g. in communication),

---

[25] Walker, T., *Managing lease portfolios*, John Wiley & Sons, Inc., Hoboken, New Jersey, 2006, page. 17.

- *Price change* – represents price changes to the various inputs and outputs in production, and
- *Inflation* – increases in the equipment price at which it can be sold in the future.

There are three reference values for measuring this risk – the concluded residual value in transactions, the estimated fair-market value at the moment of risk measuring and the historical average that was obtained by selling the equipment at the end of the leasing contract. The *Concluded residual value* represents the value of the equipment at the end of the leasing contract that the lessee estimated when booking the given lease. For the accounting aspect, income based on leasing is booked through the duration of the leasing with the assumption that the future value will be achieved. Any deviation from the booked value represents the risk. The *fair-market value* represents the estimated value of the equipment in the future. The fair-market value is not the precisely determined value, but a range of different values. The *historical average* represents the average price based on which the specific equipment has been sold in the past.

4.2 Evaluation of the Future Value of the Equipment

In this part we will outline only some of the methods used for evaluating the future value of the equipment for leasing, without a precise explanation of the calculation method.[26] The methods are:

- Decay Curve and Volatility Valuation Model
- Statistical Valuation Model
- Behavioural Valuation Model
- Factor Valuation Model

4.2.1 Decay Curve and Volatility Valuation Model

This model of valuation of the future equipment value uses a decay curve and estimated value changes around that curve taken out from a historical series of similar prices that affect the equipment's value.

Many forecasts of the equipment value start without the expected value that is called the "*decay curve*" or the equipment's fair-market value. This curve, which does not include inflation, follows the value of the equipment through its leasing service life. This curve includes possibilities of equipment damage, expected future

---

[26] For details see: Walker, T., Managing lease portfolios, John Wiley & Sons, Inc., Hoboken, New Jersey, 2006., str. 17-47.

supply and demand for the equipment, and technological changes. Also, in the curve are often included amendments by valuer or equipment manufacturer.

After the given curve is determined, it is necessary to include changes of value around that curve. Naturally, it is assumed that the leasing companies do not have historical prices for all the types of equipment, and in that case the source of such data, i.e. value change, are indexes of historical prices by equipment manufacturers. The last step is determining the distribution value change.

4.2.2 Statistical Valuation Model
The estimated future value of the equipment with this model is determined based on its own historical data that relate to the prices at which the equipment was sold at the end of the leasing contract or on the basis of external data by stockholders or industrial specialists. The basic required data in this model are: equipment type, manufacturer name, model name and serial number, year of production, starting equipment value, year of sale, sale price, side to which the equipment was sold and similar.

4.2.3 Behavioural Valuation Model
Besides the basic data that are used for evaluating the future value of the equipment, this model looks at the behaviour of the leasing recipient at the end of leasing contract, e.g. whether the recipient will buy the given equipment after the lease expires, whether it will be returned to the leasing company or the leasing contract will be renewed. Information relating to the behaviour of the leasing recipient in this model is also combined with particular statistical techniques, so the future value of the equipment and risk can be evaluated. Basic data used in this model are: probability of individual outcomes, distribution around probability of individual outcomes, incomes per each outcome, distribution around incomes, discount rate and similar.

4.2.4 Factor Valuation Model
The estimated future equipment value with this model has been determined by observing the relationship between historical prices of equipment and relevant economic factors. This model is particularly useful for long-term forecasts.

As per outlined the leasing company, besides the conventional methods of determination of equipment value, should make an effort to develop its own methodology for evaluation the future equipment value, and in accordance with the models shown.

5   Management of Collection Process and Monitoring Leasing Portfolios

In order to adequately manage the assets, as well as achieve the profitability targets, leasing companies, in the situation of general insolvency, have to develop an efficient system of receivables collection, i.e. a system of efficiently acquiring a leasing subject/collateral and a system for its sale.

The collection process needs to be supported by an automatic calculation of the lateness days, and an automatically updated list of lateness and outstanding amounts. Furthermore, within the collection process the work processes and collection activities need to be clearly separated per lateness maturity, as well as per responsibility of collection activities and results.

Collection activities consist of a regular audit of records on the full insurance required for leasing company benefit, and measures and activities for their extension.

A collection system with automatically generated lateness lists, needs to at least obtain the following functionality:

–   Automatically generated outstanding amounts towards collection processes,
–   Automatically generated reports on matured liabilities to regions, advisers/associates, type of product and other,
–   Reports on observing costs for reserves in relation to *bench-marks*,
–   Reports on collection activities and collection results,
–   Reports on portfolio migration,
–   Reports for portfolio without income, on the relationship and value of the leasing subject that is (or are not) in the possession of the leasing company.

5.1   Process of Forced Collection

Forced collection would need to commence at the latest between the 90th and 180th day of lateness. This implies activities whose priorities depends on the estimated value of the leasing subject and the probability of reimbursement of receivables, using remaining insurance instruments for leasing receivables.

The process of forced collection starts with an evaluation of the market value of the leasing subject based on the current internal methodology that we discussed earlier in this paper. If, after the evaluation of the leasing subject value has been performed, as per current internal methodology, it is determined that the value of the leasing subject is greater then receivables towards the leasing recipient, in accordance with the concluded contract, it is necessary to immediately activate the procedure for repossessing the leasing subject.

In order to protect the leasing subject, it is necessary to follow the implementing programme to find the leasing subject (e.g. for motor vehicles: electronic tracing by GPS system).

Before repossessing the leasing subject the written notice for termination of the contract for the leasing service needs to be sent to the client.

Additionally, the office for collection needs to assure the efficient process of obligatory collection by blocking the client's accounts with other financial institutions and protesting the bond of exchange and warranties given by third parties. These activities are performed as priority before the leasing subject is repossessed when:

- The estimated market value of the leasing subject is lower than the amount of the total leasing company's receivables,
- The client is already blocked by some other financial institution and/or his/her credit rating is significantly exposed to risk and/or there is a liquidation process against the client and/or client has an irregular credit history and is late making payments by over 90 days to other trustees (based on data from the Central Credit Registry – CRK),
- The collection officer estimated that the faster effect of the collection can be made by an account blockade and bill of exchange protest.

The necessary reprograms and restructuring of the leasing transactions, especially for legal entities have to be driven by risk management function. The analysis itself needs to consist of detailed projected future cash flow of the client, as a primary source of payment, as well as the choice of the most efficient strategy for the recovery of the unprofitable receivables based on the estimated Net Present Value of the cash flow and assessment of the implementation of the recovery strategy.

If the estimated market value is lower then the overdue receivable, activities of compulsive collection should be continued, based on other insurance instruments which also include possible legal actions.

Besides a well-planned collection system, monitoring and repossession of the subject, leasing companies do not solve their problem of final collection by selling the leasing subject. In that sense the method of sale could be significantly improved. Considering the significant impairment of the collection, in B&H it should be based on experiences from almost all developed European countries and as soon as possible, by establishing a system of public auctions for leasing subjects.

Organisation of auctions originates from Germany where auto fairs practically do not exist and most used vehicles are sold through auctions. Cars at auctions are mostly owned by leasing houses, rent-a-car companies, banks, importers, traders of new and used vehicles and government offices. As sellers, they determine the starting price that is usually significantly lower than the market, and pays for the vehicle's entry to the auction.

6   Management of Reserves for Losses from Leasing Business

In the middle of 2009 the Agency for FB&H banking made a decision on the minimum level and method of forming, managing and maintaining reserves for losses and risk management of leasing companies. This decision, although contradictory in some parts, specifies the calculation of the basis as the difference of the total receivables (accrued + not accrued) and the vehicle's market.

Reserve for potential losses from leasing business = Base of reserve level x reserve rate

Rate of minimum percentages of calculated reserves for potential losses from leasing business are different depending on whether the leasing subject is in the possession of the company or not.

The leasing company is obligated to monthly forms minimum reserves for losses based on financial leasing by applying the criteria of day of lateness in payments and for each group it allocates reserves for loss coverage charged to expenses in accordance with the table[27]:

Days of lateness	Reserve rate	
	Movables	Fixed items
0-60 days	0.5 %	0.5 %
61-90 days	10 %	10 %
91-180 days	50 %	50 %
over 180 days	100 %	75 %
over 360 days	-	100 %

---

[27]   Decision: on minimum level and method of forming, managing and maintaining reserves for losses and risk management of leasing companies (Based on Article 61. of the Law on leasing, Board of Directors of Agency for FB&H banking, at the meeting held on 24 June 2009).

Basis for calculation of reserve level for financial leasing contracts includes amount of total receivables (not accrued principle + accrued receivables) minus the amount of estimated market value of leasing subject.

> Principle of loss reserve level =
> (Total not accrued receivables + accrued receivables) –
> Market value of collateral of theleasing subject[28]

This calculation of the base for forming reserves approach does not take into consideration the risk factor as weighted coverage of subsequent possible risks:

- Risk of coming into the possession of the leasing subject,
- Risk of cost increase for storage /lagers,
- Risk for cost increase of the leasing subject sale,
- Risk of possible additional decrease of market value (by depreciation or changes to market conditions).

Analysing deficiencies of the above-mentioned approaches, and in order to improve the methodology and more adequate risk management of leasing companies, we suggest further processing of the method shown for reserve calculation that takes into consideration following factors:

- Internally developed system of decreasing values of leasing subject regardless of formal minimum standards (i.e. above formal minimum standards),
- Risk-factor collateral/leasing subject realisation, and
- Reserve percentage at the higher level than minimally assigned depending on whether the leasing subject is in possession of the company or not.

Basis for this calculation method of the reserve level for financial leasing contracts can be calculated based on the following formula:

> Principle of loss reserve level =
> (Total not accrued receivables + accrued receivables) –
> Material value of collateral / leasing subject

"Total not accrued receivables" represents the amount of the not accrued principle and by the leasing service contract determined compensations, and "accrued receivables" represents the sum of the accrued principle, regular and penalty interest and

---

[28] To form the reserve base, the market value of the collateral/leasing subject will be determined in accordance with the current tables on the decrease of the value of fixed items that have been used by authorised customs bodies from B&H.

all unpaid compensations determined by the leasing contract. In this case the "material collateral value" would be equal to the current market value minus the risk rate.

Therefore, the "material collateral value" would represent the collateral value that includes the estimate of its market value and risk-factor (that includes internally determined risk rate from coming into possession or realisation) and additional decrease of collateral/leasing subject market value during the sale.

> Material collateral value = current market value– risk factor of market value

Reserve rate /Risk factor	
Movables	Fixed items
Cars: 20 % Other (trucks, buses, machines…): 30 %	In urban zones: 30 %* In rural zones: 50 %*

*Higher amounts of risk factor for fixed items are the consequence of unrealistic estimates by local assessors

"Market value of collateral" (estimated value of collateral by authorised party), represents the real marketable value of leasing subject, based on relationship of current offer and demand. For movables as the basis for market value the invoiced/purchase value of movables without VAT (apart from passenger vehicles) is used, minus the amount of depreciation or internally relevant normative values of the decrease (minimally in accordance with the decreasing value of the fixed items, that is used by authorised customs bodies in B&H).

> Reserves for potential losses from leasing business =
> Principle of loss reserve level x risk rate

The leasing company is obliged to complete monthly forms for minimum reserves for losses based on operative leasing by applying the criteria days of lateness in payment and for each group it allocates reserves for loss coverage charged to costs in accordance with the elements outlined in table:

Days of lateness	Reserve rate
0-60 days	0.05 %
60-90 days	0.5 %
90-180 days	10 %
180-270 days	30 %
270-360 days	50 %
over 360 days	100 %

In case of non-payments on the 90th day, the process of forced collection starts. The advisor for the sale of the leasing service sends the request to initiate the procedure of forced collection to the Sector for risk management. We have previously mentioned this process of forced collection.

For this type of leasing it is particularly important to provide ongoing monitoring of the market value and its valuation in the context of its book value, primarily for early prevention of possible losses in cases when the market value is, because of a fall in aggregate demand, significantly below the book value, which can cause a loss for leasing companies. This particularly relates to equipment where no secured secondary market exists, which implies the importance of the primary risk evaluations based on the real repayment ability of the leasing applicant.

7   Conclusion

With the emergence and development of the global financial crisis, leasing companies have faced various problems. One of the most important is that leasing companies can not base their business primarily on the existence of a developed secondary leasing subject market.

That has, with the generally worsening financial situation and collection, caused leasing companies to change the basic strategy of risk management, and has brought them closer to the working methods of a commercial bank.

This situation has imposed on leasing companies the development of a new concept of risk management that focuses on:

1. the development of a well-planned management system for approving leasing services with the support of integrated decision-making tools,
2. the establishment of the determination processes and an assessment of the leasing subject value,

3. the development of an efficient monitoring system for leasing portfolios with established mechanisms of collection activities and repossession of leasing subjects, and

4. an automated system for forming and maintaining reserves for losses, based on a more sophisticated system and methodology, from those assigned by the minimum standards in B&H.

Literature

Bessis, Joel, *Risk Management in Banking*, John Wiley & Sons, 2003.

Hadžić, F. and Softić, A., *Significance and role of monitoring credit portfolio in function of reducing risks in financial crises conditions*, Collection of papers 12. International symposium of Association of accountants and internal auditors FB&H, Neum, October, 2009.

Decision from Agency for banking of FB&H on minimal level and method of forming, management and maintenance of reserves for losses and leasing companies risk management, June 2009

Rose S. Piter, *Management of commercial banks*, IV edition, Mate, Zagreb, 2003.

Company Culture is Worth the Cost

By Sergey Martynov (SUEK – Siberian Coal Energy Company)

Company culture is a precious asset, even if it is not included in financial reports, and helps to generate value for a company: it should therefore be audited, just like all other company processes

In recent decades, some items that are not normally included on a company's balance sheet have assumed an ever-growing role in businesses, becoming just as important as other assets. One of these is company culture, the set of beliefs, rules and intellectual (and sometimes spiritual) values shared by the majority of an organisation's employees.

1   The Importance of Company Culture

Company culture is the main means of establishing employee loyalty and its role has grown considerably, particularly in the current times of crisis. Employees represent the main asset and, at the same time, the main threat for a company's business. For example, a number of studies show that company losses caused by employee disloyalty are three times greater than those caused by unfair competition or mass-media hostility.

First of all, it is important to understand that company culture is a distinctive asset of an organisation. For example, if we decided one day to change our employees and hire new staff from other entities, the company would continue to exist, but the company culture would disappear immediately. The buildings, licences, technologies, documents and techniques would continue to exist, but something intangible, which does not appear in the company's financial reports, would vanish.

"A widespread company culture gives rise to a motivated approach to work and active participation in carrying out control procedures"

Company culture plays a fundamental role in guaranteeing success and in the efficiency of a business, for various reasons.

Firstly, it results in increased employee loyalty towards the company. A high level of employee loyalty contributes to increasing the security of company information.

However, there is no means of prevention that can stop information from being deliberately revealed, deleted or altered by employees, and the only effective way of guaranteeing the security of this information is to ensure that the company's employees remain loyal.

Secondly, a widespread company culture gives rise to a motivated approach to work and active participation in carrying out control procedures. If employees are motivated and understand the need for and importance of control procedures, they will help to reduce the number of accidents caused by negligence. The impact of a good company culture is therefore an increase in the general level of safety of the business.

Finally, company culture may result in a reduction in staff costs, thanks to a reduction in staff turnover and the costs of hiring and keeping staff: if there is a low level of company culture, employees are prepared to change jobs even for a small salary increase.

2   Development of Company Culture

While in some organisations company culture is created and grows spontaneously, in others it is deliberately promoted and developed for specific purposes. In any case, company culture within an organisation goes through various stages of development (see figure 1).

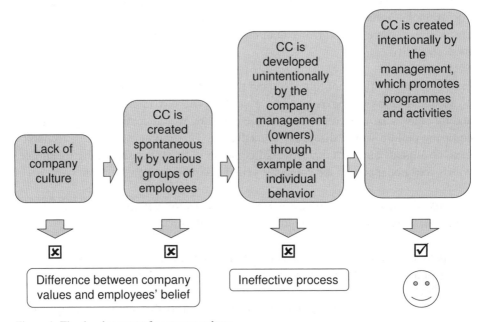

Figure 1: The development of company culture

The first stage is the lack of company culture. This is what happens mainly in recently created organisations, in which the employees, with their own values and beliefs, come from various different entities. In these situations it is extremely important for the management to make an effort to rapidly develop a new company culture, so as not to run the risk that this may be established by uncontrolled factors, such as through groups of employees from other sectors who maintain their previous culture, or by certain people asserting themselves as informal leaders.

In some cases company culture is created through the behaviour, values and beliefs illustrated by the senior managers, even unintentionally, in their relationship with the employees. The results can be positive, but the process of establishing a company culture by example may take a long time. It is extremely important, however, for the management to understand the need to develop its own culture and to put in place a programme of activities involving the employees, for example by creating specific events or occasions to promote the company values.

3   Maslow's Pyramid

But how can we encourage employees to share the company values and to become convinced supporters of them? Based on experience, we can state that a company culture can be created only when basic, social and esteem needs are satisfied. We can better understand the individual needs that influence personal motivation at work and loyalty towards en employee's company by examining American psychologist H. Maslow's "pyramid of needs" (see figure 2). In this model, the first level of needs is represented by primary needs, such as the need to sleep, personal safety etc. When the primary needs are satisfied, an individual aspires to satisfy the needs of the next level up, social needs, which can be summed up in two categories: the need to belong, that is, the need to belong to a strong social group, and the need for esteem, which is the need to be recognised by one's own social group.

The organisation must represent a strong and prestigious social group for its employees, and in order for this to happen it must know how to satisfy the individual needs of its employees. The management must also know how to value its workers on a professional level, as well on a personal level, so as to prevent any of them from seeking recognition and support by belonging to other social groups (religious or political groups, for example) and to prevent the company from becoming nothing more than a place of 'compulsory residence' for its employees, who will certainly not share or defend its values as a result. It is also extremely important to ensure that there is a relationship between the achievement of company objectives and the satisfaction of the social needs of each employee. For example, in a comparison between teams of miners who extract coal from deep mines, the team that shows the greatest productivity should receive recognition from the organisation, and it is essential that each member of the team feels that he is sharing in the recognition for his work.

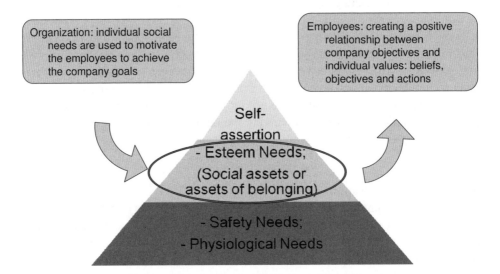

Figure 2: Maslow's pyramid

4   Internal Audit and Company Culture

Company culture can be considered to be an indicator of a business's success. In fact, a number of studies show that organisations that have a strong company culture are more successful than those whose company culture is present to a lesser extent. The positive effects on profit growth, asset value, capitalisation and other financial indicators derived from the establishment of a company culture will be far greater than the costs incurred in order to develop it: it is therefore a factor that should be taken into consideration by the internal audit, just like all other significant company processes, providing an objective and independent assessment of the degree of convergence between the company values and the employees' beliefs. The internal audit must aim to assess the effectiveness of the activities carried out by the management with a view to creating a company culture and point out the weaknesses of these activities. The result of the audit is the objective valuation of the company culture and the drawing up of recommendations to increase its effectiveness.

As for all other process reviews, when assessing the degree of company culture the internal audit must focus on three main areas: the process, the results and the dynamics.

When assessing the process, the following questions must be answered:

– What is the company doing to develop company culture?
– What is the level of coordination and control of this process?
– Are the steps for the development of company culture actually implemented?

In the majority of cases the implementation of this element is not very well developed, and is limited to a formal context for the purposes of writing reports.

When assessing the results of the process of developing company culture, the questions that need to be dealt with are:

– Are the employees satisfied socially?
– Are they proud to belong to the company?
– Are they satisfied with the recognition of their achievements?

In order to answer these questions it will be necessary to subject the employees to questionnaires developed by experts.

Finally, when assessing the dynamics of the process of developing company culture, we must take into account the degree of change compared with the past: the innovations integrated into the company culture by the management, the change in the relationship between company and employees, the level of employee loyalty, the level of motivation compared with the previous period. In conclusion, we must answer the question: has the company culture improved over the last year? Through this procedure, the company culture audit enables us to answer the question: to what extent do the employees share the company values? The range of possible results can be subdivided into five levels:

1. the employees are opposed to the company (the interests of the company and those of the employees are poles apart: lack of company culture)
2. the employees do not observe any correlation between their interests and those of the company
3. the connection between company and personal objectives is represented only by material recognition
4. the employees associate the achievement of their personal objectives, for the next two or three years, with the achievement of the company objectives. Fur-

thermore, the employees do not exclusively take material factors into consideration

5. the employees share the company values fully and are convinced supporters of them.

In every organisation there are employees who can be placed into each of the five categories. There is usually a minority of employees in the groups at either extreme, whereas the majority fall into the categories in the middle. The level of company culture is considered to be normal when the peak of distribution is in level 4 and no less than 70 % of the scores are between levels 3 and 5. The actual assessments are situated between these extreme points.

5   A Concrete Case

We carried out a test within SUEK, comparing the level of company culture with two significant indicators, the salary level, represented in figure 3, and the results of the coal production plan, represented in figure 4. We carried out the test at five different industrial plants located in the same region and characterised by similar sizes, technical equipment and business types (coal extraction industry). Around 70 employees took part in the test for each plant (10 % of the total).

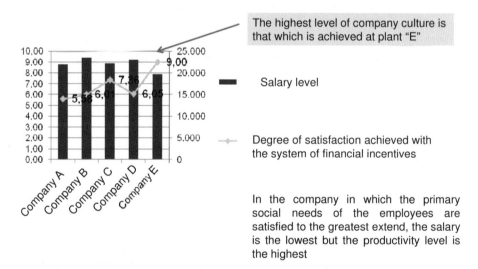

Figure 3: Company culture and salary levels

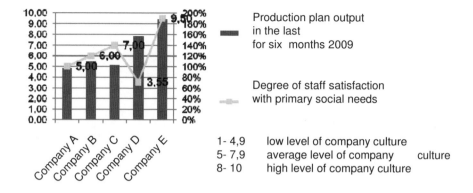

Production plan output in the last for six months 2009

Degree of staff satisfaction with primary social needs

1- 4,9	low level of company culture
5- 7,9	average level of company culture
8- 10	high level of company culture

Figure 4: Company culture and production plan

The test revealed that at plant "E", where the highest level of company culture was recorded, the average wage is lower, but the output of the production plan is higher compared with the other similar plants.

Of course, this test has no statistical value, but it is interesting all the same, because it illustrates the potential of a good company culture.

6   Final Observations

Finally, it may be useful to summarise some of the lessons we learnt during our company culture audit:

- not everyone is capable of adapting to new value systems when changing from one work environment to another, and this characteristic should be assessed during the job interview
- the process of creating a company culture takes time: it may take two or three years for the first results to be appreciated
- company culture is the most profitable long-term economic investment: minimum investment, maximum return
- there are occasional factors that may influence the results of individual tests; these factors must be monitored during the preparation stage of the audit
- in the same organisation, different functions may present different levels of company culture. In the case of multinational organisations, the companies' cultural, religious and ethnic peculiarities must be taken into account
- people must be trained to carry out surveys for the company culture audit, reducing the influence of "desirable" responses.

Governance Works, in Principle

By Neil Baker

The financial crisis has exposed poor corporate governance practice in the banking sector, but does that mean the UK's corporate governance framework needs to change, asks Neil Baker.

When the leaders of the G20 nations met in Washington in November to discuss the impact of the credit crunch, they made it clear that financial firms will face much tougher regulation in future. "We must lay the foundation for reform to help to ensure that a global crisis, such as this one, does not happen again," their end of summit communiqué said. There was little detail about how they would actually achieve this; more plans are promised for the end of March.

But the general point was clear: there had been a systematic failure, so "the system" needed to be fixed. Perhaps surprisingly, the G20 had very little to say about standards of corporate governance in the financial sector. There was much talk about the need for banks to improve their modelling and their risk management practices, to re-examine their internal controls, and to disclose more about risks. But there was only a fleeting mention of the need to improve governance. This is despite the fact that all of these specific criticisms of banking behaviour can be traced back to a failure of board-level corporate governance.

Doesn't that mean that the system of corporate governance – which in the UK means the *Combined Code of Corporate Governance* – has failed too, and therefore needs to be fixed?

1   Wrong Question?

The Financial Reporting Council, which is responsible for the Code, says not. Its chief executive, Paul Boyle, argued in a recent speech that "the primary questions should not be about the standards of corporate governance in these institutions but rather the practice of it... The focus should be on whether the existing standards have been observed in practice." The Code, for example, says that a company's board should "provide entrepreneurial leadership of the company within a framework of prudent and effective controls which enables risk to be assessed and managed." It goes on to say that non-executive directors "should satisfy themselves on the integrity of financial information and that financial controls and systems of risk management are robust and defensible." Some bank boards have arguably failed to meet either of those principles. But that doesn't mean the principles are wrong, Boyle argued.

If it is the practice, rather than the code, of corporate governance that is at fault, what should be done? The governance consultancy Independent Audit recently convened a meeting of 120 chairmen, chief executives and directors from FTSE 100 and 250 companies to discuss that question. "There has been a failure of governance, and that really centres on nonexecutives," concluded Ken Olisa, chairman of Independent Audit. The government's new City minister, Lord Myners, said that boards were "part of the problem" and needed to be strengthened. Myners called on investor groups, such as the Association of British Insurers and the National Association of Pension Funds, to provide better training and guidance for nonexecutives.

2   Non-Executive Failure?

The UK's corporate governance system is hinged on the effectiveness of nonexecutive directors. They are meant to perform the role that Walter Bagehot described for the monarchy: to be consulted, to encourage and to warn. But too often, they ask the difficult questions only when things have started to go badly. Delegates at the Independent Audit event wanted to see the performance of non-executives improve. They called for clearer selection criteria, so that better directors are appointed in the first place. They wanted them to get more training. And they suggested some quick fixes, such as holding informal meetings outside the confines of the traditional boardroom – to make it easier for nonexecutives to raise a challenge – and a ban on PowerPoint presentations at board meetings, so that people had to actually engage with each other.

But perhaps the corporate governance model asks too much of non-executives? They are on a hiding to nothing. If the business thrives, the executives make more money – in salaries, bonuses and on their share options. But the non-executives don't. Yet if the business falters, they catch as much flack as the executive directors, sometimes even more. They get none of the upside and all of the downside. This wasn't such a problem when holding a non-executive role at a bank or FTSE company was a cushy number. But increased regulation and corporate governance reform has massively increased the workload and responsibility burden of the typical non-executive. No wonder companies say it is becoming more difficult to find good candidates – a problem that the current crisis will only make worse.

Non-executive directors shouldn't shoulder all of the blame. Institutional shareholders also have a crucial role to play in corporate governance, yet their engagement with companies on governance issues tends to be poor.

With a few notable exceptions, they have been unwilling to invest in developing their ability to monitor and challenge governance practices, lapsing instead into mindless box-ticking.

3   What About Management?

And what of senior executive and management performance? A recent report from an all-party parliamentary committee, established "to develop and enhance the understanding of corporate governance", pointed to a "surprising lack of board level contact between senior managers and directors." It argued that over the last decade, the proportion of the board composed of hands-on, executive directors had declined to the point where they now account for less than a third of all board members in the FTSE 350. Yet over the same period, many of these companies have witnessed a significant increase in the size and complexity of their businesses.

These two trends have increased the responsibilities of the senior managers who sit just below board level, such as the directors responsible for human resources and information technology and the chief risk officer. In a typical FTSE 100 company, the members of parliament found, nearly half the executive committee is not represented on the main board. HR directors, for example, had a board seat at only 6 % of FTSE 350 companies. The report concluded that these people, who slip below the governance radar, are the ones who really run UK plc. Philip Dunne, the Tory MP who chairs the all-party group, said companies need to "provide shareholders with more confidence in the capabilities and skills of key executives below board level."

There is another reason why these executives need to be more involved in corporate governance. The Senior Supervisors Group, which represents financial sector regulators in France, Germany, Switzerland, the UK and the US, warned recently about the risk of companies fracturing into "organisational silos" based on highly technical management functions.

Poorly run companies often "lacked an effective forum in which senior business managers and risk managers could meet to discuss emerging issues frequently; some lacked even the commitment to open such dialogue," it said. The financial firms that had the best control over their balance sheet growth and liquidity needs were those that "demonstrated a comprehensive approach to viewing firm-wide exposures and risk, sharing quantitative and qualitative information more effectively across the firm and engaging in more effective dialogue."

There was a risk of disconnect, the group said, between the people effectively running the company and the board-level directors to whom governance principles apply. Jaap Winter, the Dutch law professor whose ideas have been behind much of the European Union's approach to corporate governance over the last decade, has talked recently about the need to make such senior managers – indeed, all employees – more accountable and responsible, rather than creating more board-level rules and regulations. Winter told the annual conference of the European Confederation of Institutes of Internal Audit (ECIIA), held recently in Berlin, that errant human behaviour caused financial crises, not flawed systems. "No system has ever generated a crisis," he said. "The first reaction is that the system has failed so we need new rules. We ask for more rules and more enforcement, but we forget about our own behaviour."

4 No Responsibility

Winter said increased regulation of financial firms and general corporates was leading to the "self-enforcement" of a compliance culture. There were already far too many rules for regulators to monitor and enforce, so they were outsourcing that work to companies themselves, he argued. This growth in corporate compliance was having a pernicious effect: crowding out personal responsibility. "It is not helping us, it makes things worse," he argued. "What compliance is doing is making sure people follow rules. We forget about our own responsibility for our behaviour and replace it with responsibility for compliance."

What are the implications for internal audit? In the short term, there is no room for complacency. Effective internal audit is a key pillar of the corporate governance framework, so if governance practice has been poor, internal auditors – like board directors, non-executives, shareholders and senior managers – should ask whether they could have done more.

"If the role of the internal auditor is to provide assurance to boards that risks are properly and effectively managed, we need to prepare to ask ourselves some serious questions," says Institute President Philip Ratcliffe. "The most basic objective of risk management is not protection of profitability, or operating effectively and efficiently; it is survival. And major institutions, doubtless with well-staffed internal audit departments, and boards which gave serious contemplation to the demands of good governance and risk management, have almost overnight gone to the wall."

Internal auditors in the financial sector should ask themselves whether they were looking at the right risks, says Ratcliffe: "It is a lot to demand of the internal auditor that he or she should challenge the locally-accepted wisdom. However, that is what our profession demands – the ability and willingness to challenge the status quo and to say the unsayable."

Looking to the future, there is a clear role for internal auditors in helping their organisations to fix the poor governance practices that caused or at least exacerbated the crisis. If non-executive directors are lacking information and asking the wrong questions, for example, or if the board cannot grasp an organisation-wide view of risk, internal audit can help. Indeed, the internal audit profession has been asking organisations to take these challenges more seriously for years. Perhaps now they will be more willing to listen.

Internal Audit Practices

Contribution by Internal Audit to IT Compliance

By Thomas Lohre, MBA[29]

The constant increase in laws, ordinances, norms, standards, contracts, guidelines, etc. leads to intransparency in companies regarding the legal provisions and regulations to be complied with. This results in considerable, latent uncertainty regarding the risk of possible rule violations. The avoidance of such risks by ensuring adherence to provisions is the objective of corporate compliance and in IT specifically, IT compliance. Internal audit can make a valuable contribution to this, as it can objectively assess the IT compliance efforts in companies through its specialist knowledge, methodical knowledge and independence, thereby assisting in the prevention of rule violations. Furthermore, it can assist in IT compliance adding value to the company by providing valuable information.

1   Introduction

Corporate governance, risk management, compliance. All of these are concepts that can no longer be imagined away from the current business vocabulary and academic literature and are on everyone's lips.[30] Perhaps even enriched with the concept of IT? In fact, in recent times, IT has increasingly developed into a competitive factor, which makes a crucial contribution to the implementation of corporate strategies. Furthermore, it accounts for a considerable portion of the costs and investments and the legal and regulatory requirements for IT have also grown significantly.[31]

Corporate Governance is a concept originating from Anglo-American vocabulary[32] and has, since then, been used for the debate regarding proper business management.

---

[29]   Thomas Lohre, MBA, Graduate in Business Administration/Graduate in Business Information Technology, CISA, CISM, IT Auditor at DATEV eG. This article reflects the author's personal opinion.

[30]   In order to no longer debate the relationships between IT, governance and compliance in such a differentiated manner, Teubner/Feller suggest a summarised view. This would result in a single, complex problem area, which would only need to be analysed from different perspectives. Cf. Teubner/Feller (2008), p. 407.

[31]   Cf. Heier/Maistry (2008), p. 93.

[32]   The attempt to produce a translation into German has not taken place so far. As Becker/Ulrich correctly note, the concept has its origin in Latin and is derived from the term, "gubernare", which means regulate, manage or control.

Corporate governance generally encompasses the entirety of all international and national principles for good and responsible business management, which applies to the employees, as well as the management of companies. Corporate governance is not an internationally standardised body of rules and regulations, but rather, with the exception of a few internationally accepted, common rules, they are a country-specific understanding of responsible business management.[33] An important milestone for Germany was the adoption of the DCGK (German Corporate Governance Code) by a government commission in February 2002, last amended on 6 June 2008 by the government commission.[34] However, in addition to country-specific corporate governance provisions, cross-national, industry-specific versions also exist.

Corporate governance is very complex and encompasses compulsory and voluntary measures: adherence to legal provisions and regulations (compliance[35]), the observance of accepted standards and recommendations and the development of and adherence to company guidelines.[36] Another aspect of corporate governance is the structuring and setting-up of management and control structures.

Characteristics of good corporate governance are:

– Functioning business management
– Preserving the interests of various parties (e.g. the stakeholders)
– Targeted cooperation between business management and business monitoring
– Transparency in the corporate communication
– Appropriate handling of risks
– Management decisions are aimed at long-term value enhancement

The German code does not create any new legal standards, but rather, reproduces legal provisions in a legible and abbreviated form and issues recommendations and

---

[33] One of these internationally accepted bodies of rules and regulations is the COSO Framework. COSO basically defined internal controls as one process, which is initiated by top management or other persons in the organisation and is aimed, inter alia, at adequate security in the field of "compliance with relevant laws and regulations". The COSO Framework is also regarded as the relevant framework for the fulfilment of the requirements of Section 404 of the Sarbanes-Oxley Act.

[34] See DCGK (2007). For the effects of the German Corporate Governance Code on the financial statement audit, see IDW PS 345.

[35] The term can be translated with "compliance, adherence to rules". Schneider accurately determines that it is a "truism" that companies and governing bodies need to act in accordance with valid law, even if this is now called "compliance".

[36] According to von Hehn/Hartung, two different bundles of measures result from this definition. On the one hand, measures to ensure legal conduct and, on the other hand, measures for early identification and minimisation of risks. Relevant details cf. von Hehn/Hartung (2006), p. 1909 f.8 cf. Theusinger/Liese (2008), p. 1420.

suggestions. Nevertheless listed companies must comply with this code. With the "declaration of compliance" pursuant to Article 161 AktG (German Companies Act), the management board and supervisory board establish, on an annual basis, whether the recommendations of the Corporate Governance Code have been complied with or if deviations have occurred.

IT compliance is represented by risk management, data protection, IT security, legally compliant archiving and legally compliant IT implementation.

Even if a comparable legal regulation does not exist for the management of a GmbH (limited liability company), Article 43 Par. 1 GmbHG (Limited Liability Companies Act), obligates the management to apply the due care and diligence of a prudent merchant in company matters.[37] To this extent, the Corporate Governance Code also radiates its effects onto the management of a GmbH. Since January 1st 2009, the Law on the Modernisation of Company Annual Accounts (BilMoG) has expanded the group to include companies that have issued securities on the stock exchange.

The KonTraG (Law on Control and Transparency in the Corporate Sector) is of key importance, which, inter alia, resulted in the regulation of Article 91 Par. 2 AktG (German Companies Act). Through this, the duty exists to undertake precautions against risks that threaten the company's existence. The requirements of Section 404 of the Sarbanes Oxley Act (SOX) for the establishment of an internal control system and the BilMoG, regarding reporting on the internal control system and risk management system regarding the financial reporting process, have a similar objective.

The task of compliance[38], as part of corporate governance, is adherence to voluntary and binding regulations and laws. IT compliance, as a subordinated category of compliance/corporate governance, describes responsible and legally valid handling of the information technology existing in the company and deals with adherence to legal provisions or other directives, which need to be considered within the IT landscape. It can therefore be understood as an element of functioning risk management within a company, whereby risk management generally has the aim of effectively

---

[37] Cf. basic comment by Damken (2007). Regarding the development of corporate governance in Germany and its density of regulations, see the comments of Funk/Rossmanith/Alber (2006).

[38] In the literature, there is now a distinction between "compliance in the wider sense" and "compliance in the narrower sense". With the former, it involves, as already mentioned, compliance with all regulations that result from legal provisions, regulations and internal specifications. The latter term originates from the new academic contributions and is understood as the ethical guidelines that globally active company usually give themselves within the context of more intensively propagated corporate social responsibility. See the comments of Cauers/Haas/Jakob/Kremer/Schartmann/Welp (2008), p. 2717.

and efficiently identifying, assessing and managing risks (as a probability of occurrence of a negative event multiplied by the financial scale). In this respect, IT compliance addresses risks that result from IT not functioning as planned, being deficiently organised, not being operating or secured in accordance with provisions, etc., so that legal provisions or other rules and regulations are not, or only deficiently fulfilled/duties of care are not given sufficient attention. This risk must be handled within the context of risk management using suitable organisational, technical and personnel measures. Internal audit should be regarded as part of the bundle of measures.

2 Elements and Regulations of IT Compliance

Before dealing with the regulations for IT compliance below, in a first step, it must be clarified, which elements IT compliance can be comprised of. In the previous section, in the definition of "IT compliance", the risks which should be addressed by IT compliance were already dealt with. This involves

- IT that does not function without errors,
- a deficient structure in the IT operation,
- IT is not operated or used as required,
- IT is not accordingly available or
- IT is not adequately backed up.

If IT compliance should be necessary, all of these risks need to be covered in the company. This then leads to IT needed to be represented by the following basic elements:

- Riskmanagement
  Are duties of care complied with in the operation of the IT infrastructure? Are the reporting and documentation duties fulfilled?
- Data protection
  Are measures undertaken against loss of data or damage to data?
- IT security
  Are mechanisms implemented to avoid unauthorised internal and external access?
- Legally compliant archiving
  Are the requirements of HGB (German Commercial Code), AO (German Tax Code), GOB (principles of proper accounting, GoBS (principles of due computer-aided accounting systems) and GDPdU (principles of data access and verifiability of digital documents) taken into account?
- Legally compliant IT implementation
  Does a correct licensing policy and licence management exist?

Four groups of legal provisions and regulations can basically be distinguished, which represent a basic overall structure for a methodical analysis of IT compliance requirements (cf. Fig. 1):

– Legal provisions, i.e. legal standards (legal provisions, as well as legal ordinances issued on the basis of these by administrations), as well as administrative regulations and other directives referred to in laws, legal ordinances and administrative regulations or that are drawn upon for the interpretation of case law;
– Contracts that a company concludes with customers, suppliers and other market participants and which contain IT-related agreements (e.g. service level agreements);
– Directives outside of the company that relate to IT, e.g. norms, standards, certificates or guidelines of diverse institutions;
– Internal company directives, which include internal specifications, such as policies, organisational or process instructions, operational level agreements (OLAs) or in-house standards, insofar as they contain IT-related specifications.

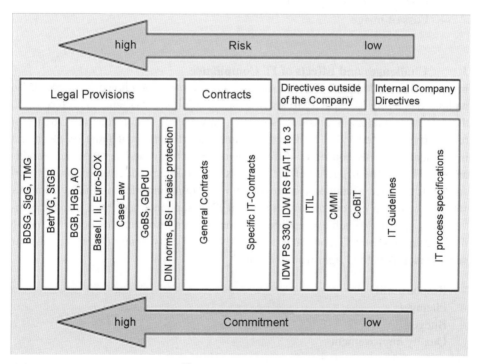

Figure 1: IT compliance directives11[39]

---

[39]   On the basis of Klotz/Dorn (2008), p. 11–14.

With legal provisions and contracts, the risks tend to be assessed as being higher, because a monetary penalty is either legally defined or contractually regulated. Also, in these cases, because of prosecuting institutions/injured contracting parties, who intend to actively pursue their interests, the probability is more likely to exist that a violation will be protested and a claim will be pursued and carried through. From the point of view of IT compliance, directives regarding risk and commitment are not as important, even if a clear distinction needs to be made. For example, directives for testing and certifications are more relevant (IDW) than regulations that are applied as "reference models" or "best practice models" (ITIL, COBIT).
The risks of deficient IT compliance can be split into: [40]

- Risks for the corporate bodies
  - Civil law liability risks
  - Criminal law risks
- Risks for the company
  - Civil law and other financial liability[41]
  - Criminal law responsibility
  - Loss of image

3 Challenges and Effects of IT Compliance

In order to fulfil legal provisions and directives, there is no choice for a company, without damaging its capacity to act or even its continued existence. A reference to these legal/regulatory necessities is correct, however it is not generally sufficient for justifying added value by IT compliance.[42] Furthermore, it must be clear that investments not only contribute differently to productivity, added value and compliance of IT, but the triggered effects can also be counterproductive. In order to resolve this conflict, a standardised approach is required, in order to initially compensate the negative effects of investments in IT compliance and then using the investment in order to achieve additional benefit. This also includes not terminating the investments after IT compliance is achieved and consistently observing the four success factors below, right from the start:[43]

- Responsibility
- Planning
- Budget
- Quality improvement

---

[40] Cf. Bachmann (2007), p. 95 f. For a detailed description also BITKOM (2005), p. 5 et seqq.

[41] This also includes exclusion or non-consideration with public tender procedures, the possible loss of insurance protection and higher refinancing costs. In detail cf. Lensdorf/Steger (2006), p. 209.

[42] In detail cf. Broadbent/Kitzis (2005).

[43] Cf. Böhm (2008), p. 20 f. for a detailed description of the four success factors listed below.

With this, the preconditions are created for maintaining the added value of IT achieved after the first-time establishment of IT compliance over the longer term, as well as raising the initially impaired performance t to a higher level than prior to establishment. Fig. 2 illustrates both situations, if, after the initiation of measures t(1), IT compliance is established t(2) and after this, investments are absent t¬C(1) or if regular monitoring and adjustment of the introduced controls and processes is carried out afterwards t¬C(2).

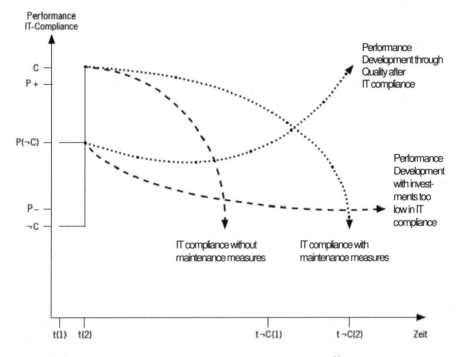

Figure 2: Comparison of the effects of IT compliance on performance[44]

When investments are absent, the efficiency of the controls can diminish, which can lead to a loss of IT compliance (¬C), e.g. through faulty changes to IT processes and IT systems. In parallel with this, the IT performance declines, because monitoring measures that have become ineffective continue to involve effort. Therefore, two disadvantageous effects add up, with negative consequences for IT compliance and IT performance. The illustration clearly shows the negative effects on performance and the faster loss of IT compliance.

Regular monitoring, adjustment and improvement slows down the degradation of controls or the effectiveness of IT systems and contributes to the reduction of nega-

---

[44] Derives from Böhm (2008), p. 21.

tive effects on the performance of IT. This requires extending the investment in IT compliance beyond the time of initial establishment, until the positive effects of IT compliance display their first impact. As can be seen in the illustration, the point in time of non-IT-compliance is reached significantly later this way t¬C(2). Furthermore, an improvement in performance takes place with a time lag, after initial negative effects. Through fewer errors, more effective IT processes and improved transparency in the entire IT operation, it is only possible to turn the effect around after a change in trend. One-off activities and investments made are ultimately futile, as many tasks arise again over time.

From the situation described here, it can be concluded that after one-off establishment of IT compliance, further measures need to be applied continuously, so that IT compliance is not only maintained, but the performance of IT is also improved. Only a combined approach, comprised of first-time establishment of IT compliance and permanent measures, leads to positive added value of IT compliance for corporate success.

4   Added value of IT compliance

On the basis of a general definition, performance is regarded as the ratio of actual output to a defined standard output, in relation to a quantity of input. Therefore, performance stands for efficiency, effectiveness and cost optimisation. The added value of IT can therefore be defined as performance increase through effective use of IT and efficient IT processes.

Does potential benefit for IT compliance result from the added value of IT and improved performance? Because legal and regulatory requirements have different emphases and place deviating, detailed requirements on IT, the advantages of IT that complies with these are also different. Below, possibilities are presented with the necessary generality, which result after covering virtually all specifications, because it essentially involves the CIA triangle (Confidential, Integrity, Availability) in relation to IT:[45]

–   Protective function: defence from penalties, conditions and loss of reputation
    Even if the benefit of IT compliance represents a significant point, it must not
    be forgotten that compliance with legal requirements primarily protects the
    company from penalties, conditions and limitations to its business activity. Disregarding legal provisions can have civil law and criminal law consequences, in
    addition to the loss of public image. Disregarding external directives does not

---

[45]   Cf. Böhm (2008), p. 26 f. and Lösler (2005), p. 104 et seqq.In his article, Lösler deals exclusively with compliance within the area of financial market law, however, his ideas can undoubtedly be transferred to companies outside of this sector and to the area of IT.

usually led to legal consequences, however, it must also be considered that loss of image can result if certifications do not run successfully.

– Quality assurance and innovation function: Elimination of deficits in the IT organisation
  The examination of the IT organisation often reveals weak points, which can be corrected within the context of the ongoing establishment of IT compliance. The correction of errors in IT processes or comparison with best practices (e.g. ITIL, COBIT) is alone already added value.

– Monitoring and supervisory function: Effective IT processes through effective controls
  Compliance with duties must be checked. It is an essential function element of IT compliance, to ensure monitoring of compliance with legal provisions and directives and set up a relevant control organisation.

– Standardisation: Reduction of variations with IT processes
  The standardised documentation of IT processes shows inevitably existing structural variations. It lends itself to carry out harmonisation, right down to the standardisation of IT processes, before the controls are implemented.

– Capacity for growth: IT compliance creates relief
  IT compliance means gaining operating dependability, reliability and stability in IT, so that less time and capacity needs to be invested in the proper operation of IT.

– Added value: Increasing company value
  The existing IT does not exclusively decide the success or failure of a corporate acquisition, however, it is undisputed that the company value is higher if the IT conforms to the valid legal provisions or directives.[46]

– Marketing function: Improving the reputation with customers and other market participants
  IT compliance contributes to maintaining a company's reputation with customers, employees, other market participants and regulatory authorities, as well as the general public and other stakeholders, as, on the one hand, negative publicity due to legal violations is avoided and, on the other hand, the company's credibility is raised in its external presentation.[47]

– Verifiability: Less preparation and shorter implementation
  With the systematic analysis of valid laws and directives, meticulous derivation of the resulting IT requirements and the development and implementation of effective controls to comply with these requirements, the company shows that it seriously aims to fulfil its duties.

As the result of establishing IT compliance, extensive, current and standardised documentation of the IT processes should exist. Applications that are critical to op-

---

[46] Cf. Böhm (2008), p. 27.

[47] Cf. Rosinus (2008), p. 261

erations and the necessary IT infrastructure for their operation are inventoried, contractual and service relationships with external service providers and analysed and IT security is increased significantly. The more complex these matters are, the higher the added value already is through these effects. Legislative conformity of IT is a necessity for a company, in order to offer services, which maintain access to the capital markets and ensure creditworthiness.

5   Promotion of IT Compliance by Internal Audit

When viewed in isolation, the fact that a company has an internal audit department is not yet a sufficient characteristic to indicate that the company observes all of the legal provisions or directives for compliance/IT compliance.[48] However in order to show that the internal audit department provides a valuable contribution to IT compliance, it will be discussed below, how internal audit can approach the subject of "IT compliance" and which approaches arise in practice.

With the considerations regarding which tasks arise in the field of IT compliance for internal audit, it must be considered how IT compliance can be integrated into the existing organisational structures. At the core, are three models exist:[49]

–   IT compliance as a department
–   IT compliance as part of the legal department
–   IT compliance as part of internal audit

While there are no special features to be taken into consideration with the audit activities of internal audit for the first two models, with the last option, it must be considered that internal audit loses its independence. This results in an independent and objective audit of IT compliance by the own internal audit department no longer be capable of being conducted. This should then take place externally – e.g. once per year by the appropriate external auditor.

5.1   Risk-oriented Auditing

Audit risk is regarded as the auditor's risk of confirming circumstances, which contain substantial misstatements, without this having been revealed by the audit.

---

[48]   Due to the limited audit assignment of internal audit, it can only promote IT compliance to a limited extent. Cf. Bertschinger (2004), p. 387.

[49]   On the basis of Cauers/Haas/Jakob/Kremer/Schartmann/Welp (2008), p. 2718. A detailed description of the different models is waivedin this article. Instead, reference is made to the cited article.

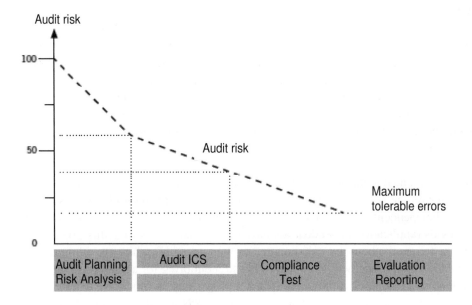

Figure 3: Audit risk with risk-oriented audit[50]

Audit risk, as such, cannot be determined on an isolated basis, but rather, is a combination of the following individual risks:

- Business risk
  Business risk is regarded as risks of a general nature, on which the activities of the companies, the business environment and the way in which they conduct their business are based.
- Control risk
  Controls risks are those risks arising from weaknesses in or failure of internal control measures. If internal controls are envisaged, but are not or only insufficiently effective, or employees do not carry out their monitoring functions, the risk of errors or irregularities arises, which cannot be revealed and corrected by the control functions built into the workflow process.
- Disclosure risk
  Disclosure risk is when risky circumstances that are not,or only insufficiently, taken into consideration in the audit object, are not discovered by the auditor.
- Inherent risk
  Inherent risk is regarded as the susceptibility of a specific audit field to significant errors or faulty transactions, which can result in a misstatement in the annual financial statement, under the assumption that no internal controls or monitoring exist, which the auditor can rely on.

---

50 Marbacher (2000), p. 1182.

With a risk-oriented audit approach, the audit first analyses the business risks, the business processes and the controls carried out in the company, as well as measures for monitoring them, within the context of the audit planning. On the basis of the result of the risk analysis, the auditor determines the "error sources" and audits these areas in a targeted manner. Fig. 3 shows the relationship between risk analysis and audit activities. It can also be seen from this that each activity of the risk-oriented auditor is aimed at reducing the audit risk. In this sense, the audit planning and risk analysis are not administration, but rather, a significant part of an effective audit.[51]

The risk-oriented audit includes the IT audit. In its audit activity, internal audit concentrates on the risk assessment in the infrastructure and central IT services (application-independent audits) and in the IT-administered accounting and business processes (application-dependent audits).[52] The results of these audits provide extensive feedback about the risk situation in the area of IT, while providing recommendations for strengthening the controls and monitoring for a risk-optimised audit programme. Therefore, a risk-oriented audit programme is conducive to IT compliance for two reasons. On the one hand, the controls and monitoring are assessed and possibly adjusted, while on the other hand, a risk assessment of IT takes place, which should also take place on an annual basis within the context of an IT compliance programme. Therefore, an additional, independent risk assessment already takes place during the year by internal audit.

5.2 Truth and Fairness Audits

When auditing truth and fairness, a comparison is carried out between two objects. This involves the audit object (actual object), on the one hand, which is compared to a desired condition (target object). The focus of this is on IT, as the aim should be to support IT compliance. The general task of a truth and fairness audit is clarified by Fig. 4. The approach by the auditor for such an audit will be based on the following procedure:[53]

- Recording the target object
- Recording the actual object
- Conducting a target-actual comparison
- Result:
    - Deviations:yes, no
    - Weak points: actual object, target object

---

[51] Cf. Marbacher (2000), p. 1182.
[52] Cf. Marbacher (2000), p. 1184.
[53] Cf. Kaiser (2008), p. 22.

– Development of recommendations:
  – Actual object
  – Target object

Risk-oriented audits, as well as truth and fairness audits, are elementary components of the daily work of internal audit and therefore simultaneously support the establishment of IT compliance. After all, with the truth and fairness audit, the IT compliance directives presented in this article are frequently the references for deriving the target objects. Therefore, it is examined, e.g. whether individual items in the annual financial statement have been correctly calculated, correct cash management exists, contracts have been properly concluded and administered, service level agreements are arranged, monitored and concluded or whether internal regulations, such as password polices, are implemented and followed.

Truth and fairness audit = target-actual comparison
Examination regarding whether and to what extent the circumstances to be audited (actual object) meets specific requirements (target object)

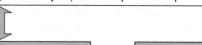

Target Objects	Actual Objects
Anchored in: • Laws • Standards • Contracts • Statutes • Audit standards • Organisational guidelines • Work instructions	**Examples:** • Workflow for purchasing processes • Awarding contracts to service providers • Cash management • Processing projects • Investment planning • Internal audit activity • Transactions with related parties • Management decision-making processes • Providing information to the supervisory board and shareholders

Figure 4: Function of a truth and fairness audit[54]

---

54 Kaiser (2008), p. 21.

5.3 The IT compliance program

A significant range of activities for internal audit within IT compliance is the review as to whether an effective IT compliance programme has been introduced/implemented in the company. In order to assess the effectiveness, it must be known, which elements an adequate IT compliance programme must be comprised of. For this, the main elements of this programme are discussed below and it is simultaneously described, how these elements need to be implemented, so that an assessment by internal audit is possible:[55]

Organisational structure

The IT compliance programme must be organised according to the size of the company, in order to adequately fulfil its functions and responsibilities. Generally, employees in different specialist areas should be involved, in order to cover the company's entire functional depth and contribute the appropriate specialist know-how. The person responsible for the programme must be provided with sufficient rights, be familiar with internal and external regulations and report to the management board. In an ideal case, all of these points should be recorded in rules of procedure for the IT compliance programme, in order to clearly define the rights and specify the duties.

Ascertainment of IT compliance risks

In addition to the initial ascertainment of the IT compliance risks at the beginning of the project, during the further course of the IC compliance programme, this ascertainment must be repeated at least once per year. The objective of this annually recurring ascertainment is to identify the directives that have the greatest effects on the company and its IT compliance efforts.

Company guidelines (code of conduct/code of ethics)

The preparation and implementation of a corporate guideline is important for successful IT compliance, which can also be found in the literature under the terms, "code of conduct" or "code of ethics".[56] These guidelines are used for regulating two important aspects: On the one hand, ethical guidelines and corporate visions – often in the form of "mission statements" – are intended to be recorded. On the other hand, the company employees are to be provided with practical instructions

---

[55] Cf. Burch (2008), p. 54 et seqq.

[56] Cf. Rosinus (2008), p. 263 f. Regarding the problem of the selectivity between the terms, "code of conduct"and "code of ethics", see also in detail Ziegleder (2007), p. 248.

on conduct for concrete situations in day-to-day company activities.[57] For internal audit, the aim is to examine the corporate vision, as well as the individual instructions on conduct, in detail.[58] Furthermore, it must be ensured that through regular reviews, the corporate guidelines are kept current and have been adapted to possibly changed legal provisions and directives.

Internal Directives

As a result of the IT compliance programme, an extensive internal directive is implemented, through which the company ensures compliance with the legal provisions and directives. In many cases, the compliance is ensured through an automated workflow, which supports the necessary audits and approvals. For internal audit, on the one hand, the entire directive is therefore of interest, which it examines regarding whether it is appropriate to the respective size of company. In the other hand, it must be investigated whether the automated workflows achieve their goal.

Sensitisation of the Employees

In order to implement the results of the IT compliance programme in the company, it is not only sufficient to change regulations, but also, the employees, who are intended to follow these regulations, must be made aware that the regulations are being introduced or changed. Training courses in this area lend themselves in order to inform the employees about their duties, while documenting to the company that the employees have been sufficiently informed about the directives. During the further course of the process, awareness campaigns lend themselves, in order to provide information about changes and maintain the sensitisation of the employees to the subject.

Internal Control System (ICS)[59]

Within the context of the IT compliance programme, controls should have been established to monitor compliance with the directives, or should be elicited through regular audits. To the extent that a requirement to adjust the controls should arise from this, it must be ensured, within an appropriate period of time, that corrective measures are undertaken. The ICS is essentially necessary due to legal regulations

---

[57] For detailed handling of this aspect, see Zieg¬leder (2007), p. 245 et seqq.

[58] Cf.in detail Meyer (2006), p. 3605.

[59] The ICS should not only be understood in the sense that it only involves the disclosure of undesired processes, but also control in terms of aspects, in the sense of structuring undesired events. Cf. the comments by Ruud/Isufi/Friebe (2008), p. 938 f., which rightly point out that the translation from English is frequently used incompletely in the literature and practice.

(Article 91 Par. 2 AktG (Companies Act)), however, in many aspects, it is also based on the IT compliance targets.[60] For internal audit, it is crucial to assess the monitoring controls and examine the results of the regular audits.

Responsibilities

Another component of effective IT compliance should be that the dual-control principle has been introduced for critical business processes and clear responsibilities have been defined within the processes. This needs to be examined in detail by internal audit. For this, it lends itself to conduct process audits and test the extent to which the specifications are complied with.

5.4 Future-oriented IT Compliance through Environmental Monitoring/Early Identification

After successful implementation of an IT compliance programme, the question subsequently arises in the company of how the intended success can be achieved/further developments can be carried out, using additional measures. As already described, after one-off establishment of IT compliance, further measures can be undertaken so that not only IT compliance is maintained, but the performance of IT is also positively influenced. The turbulence of the business environment not only leads to customer requirements, competitive conditions, market structures, technologies, etc. changing in a short period of time, but also the legal general conditions and national/international directives.[61] For IT compliance management, such environmental changes can result in the necessity to change internal regulations, processes, controls and monitoring or set up completely new regulations.[62] In all of these cases, a certain lead time is necessary, i.e. the indicated changes must be identified as early as possible, so that scope for reaction still exists. The larger this time scope is, the more valuable such changes to be carried out in the company are.

Therefore, IT compliance management must not exclusively be oriented inward, but rather, must be aware of the influencing external and internal factors and identify

---

[60] Cf. the results of the survey by Ruud/Isufi/Friebe (2008) p. 939 f., with medium-sized companies in Switzerland, according to which the ICS is also aimed at compliance targets with 79% of the companies surveyed.

[61] Weimar/Grote rightly speak about increasing judicialisation of the economy, which goes hand-in-hand with higher complexity and dynamics of the legal field of knowledge. Cf. Weimar/Grote (1997), p. 844.

[62] In contrast, law as a means of structuring and innovation research is largely neglected. Cf. the comments in Hoffmann-Riem (2008), p. 4 f. Known in the academic literature under the term "regulatory push-pull" as a source for innovations. Cf. Männer (2007).

and evaluate the emerging changes to legal provisions and directives.[63] This requires systematic monitoring of the environment, by means of which the future changes in the environment are identified at an early stage and are taken into consideration in the further development of the internal directive. Successful IT compliance that it aimed toward the future is ideally comprised of the following areas:[64]

- Regulatory early information
- Competition analysis
- Technological market research

For internal audit, this means to examine whether appropriate legal environmental monitoring takes place within the company, to what extent this process is adequate for the size of company and whether all of the areas presented here are covered by the process.

5.5 Certifications

A possibility for companies to show the customers, employees, other market participants and regulatory authorities that it is complying with legal provisions and directives, is to have itself certified. This directly supports IT compliance, because the employees actively deal with the respective valid specifications and directives and become sensitised to them. Furthermore, the marketing function of such certifications is obvious, as the probability of legal violations declines while the external presentation is positively influenced. Even if internal audit cannot directly take action in this regard, it can make sense to suggest such certifications or perform preparatory work. For the assessment by internal audit regarding which certifications[65] can be meaningful, possible testing standards and related certifications are presented below:[66]

---

[63] Cf. Jetter (2004), p. 18 f.

[64] Detailed information about the three areas is provided by Homann (2005), p. 20 et seqq.

[65] Networking can occur between the different certifications and testing standards. E.g. examination of data protection by regulatory authorities and ISO/IEC 27001 / ISO/IEC 27001 and IDW PS 330/331. Regarding detailed handling, see UIMCert (2007), p. 877.

[66] In this context, one can speed of "IT compliance audit" or "IT compliance certifications", as compliance with a directive is examined.

ISO/IEC[67] 20000

ISO/IEC 20000 is an internationally accepted standard for IT service management, in which the requirements for professional IT service management are documented. The standard is based on the process descriptions, as they are described by the IT Infrastructure Library (ITIL) of the Of¬fice of Government Commerce (OGC) and supplements these in a complementary manner. The ISO/IEC 20000 certification represents the only possibility for objectively measuring and certifying the successful implementation of IT service management on the basis of an international standard, as ITIL is not a standard and certification is not possible on this basis.

ISO/IEC 27001 (formerly BS 7799-2)

The ISO/IEC 27001 standard specifies the requirements for the establishment, introduction, operation, monitoring, maintenance and improvement of a documented information security management system under consideration of the risks within the entire organisation. Through this, requirements are specified for the implementation of suitable security measures, which are intended to be adapted to the constellations of the individual organisation.

ISO 27001 Certification on the Basis of Basic IT Protection

Together with the basic IT protection catalogues and their recommendations for standard security measures, the basic IT protection approach has now become a de facto standard for IT security. The requirement for awarding an ISO 27001 certificate on the basis of IT protection or an audit certificate is an examination of the information security management system by a BSI-certified auditor for ISO 27001 audit on the basis of basic IT protection. I.e., not only the system is examined, but also the components of the basic protection catalogues and their implementation.

ISO/IEC 9001

The ISO/IEC 9001 standard defined the requirements for a quality management system (QM system) for the case that an organisation must present its ability to provide products, which fulfil the customers' requirements and official requirements and aim to increase customer satisfaction.

---

[67] ISO (The International Organization for Standardization) and IEC (The International Electrotechnical Commission) are global organisations that deal with the standardisation of the systems. National institution that are member of ISO or IEC, also participate in the development of international standards through the so-called tech¬nical committees.

For internal audit, it is not only of interest to determine how IT compliance is implemented, but also, which accompanying measures can be secured by IT compliance over the long term.

Data Protection Audit

In order to improve data protection and data security, vendors of data processing systems and programs and data processing centres can have their data protection concept, as well as their technical facilities, inspected and assessed pursuant to Article 9a BDSG (Federal Data Protection Act), by independent and certified auditors, as well as publishing the result of the audit.

SAS 70

SAS 70 is an auditing standard that was adopted by the American Institute of Certified Public Accountants (AICPA) and is applied by auditing firms. The standard relates to the internal control system of an organisation and the proper operation of outsourced service processes, such as data centre services. In SAS 70 Type I, the internal control system of the service provider is assessed, in Type II, its effectiveness is tested. SAS 70 does not know any catalogues of measures and audits; however, SAS 70 test reports are recognised by the Sarbanes Oxley Act as a confirmation of Section 404.

Software Certificates Pursuant to IDW PS 880

This software audit is essentially a process audit with the focus of ascertaining the necessary processing functions, the correctness of program processes and the program rules, the software security and the correctness of the documentation. The guideline is based on the testing of software products with the software manufacturer or software user, prior to implementation in the software user's respective business environment. The subject matter of the software testing is the assessment of compliance with the principles of proper accounting (GoB) within the context of the processes specified by the software. The principles of due computer-aided accounting systems (GoB) specify the GoB, if the accounting takes place with the aid of computers. In the business application environment, there is unlikely to be any software that does not fall under the scope of the GoBS and therefore, the GoB. However, with these certificates, it must be taken into consideration that the proper application of the software was not the subject matter of the audit.[68]

---

[68]   Cf. Philipp (1999), p. 156.

If such certifications should already exist, this is already an indication for internal audit that the company, and ultimately the employees, consciously or unconsciously, have dealt with the subject of IT compliance or individual areas of this. Even if the company has not set up a dedicated IT compliance programme, these certifications form a good basis for further steps in the direction of achieving IT compliance. In comparison with the IT compliance directives, it is then also shown that compliance with the legal provisions or directives has already been achieved in the areas where a certification was carried out by the organisation.

6   Summary

For successful IT compliance, it is not only important to initiate a project on a one-off business and establish IT compliance. In fact, it also requires a continuous process, for permanently investing in IT compliance, so that a benefit and added value can be obtained, therefore fulfilling the IT compliance requirements over the long term and improving the performance of IT itself.

As the article has shown, how IT compliance is implemented in the company is not the only relevant point for internal audit. It is also significant, through which accompanying measures the company intends to secure the contribution of IT compliance over the long term. As presented, there are several possibilities for not only announcing this internally, but also externally. Internal audit must consider these possibilities in order to assess the IT compliance process as a whole. In order to carry out effective audits of the IT compliance programme, it will therefore be the function and duty of internal audit to remain informed about the activities carried out, on a continuing and immediate basis. Only in this way, can it examine whether new regulations are being applied correctly and IT compliance is sustainably effective. Therefore, provided that it is not directly responsible for IT compliance, the role of internal audit is to support the implementation of the IT compliance programme, examine this, provide advice, assess the measures for monitoring the legal provisions and directives and submit suggestions for improvement, if necessary.[69]

Literature

Bachmann: Compliance – Rechtliche Grundlagen und Risiken. Ein Thema (auch) für Unternehmen außerhalb der Finanzindustrie, in: Der Schweizer Treuhänder 1–2/2007, p. 93–98.

Becker/Ullrich: Corporate Governance in mittelständischen Unternehmen. Ein Bezugsrahmen, in: Zeitschrift für Corporate Governance 6/2008, p. 261–267.

Bertschinger: Zum Wirkungsgrad der Revisionsstelle in der Corporate Governance, in: Der Schweizer Treuhänder 5/2004, p. 383–388.

BITKOM: Matrix der Haftungsrisiken. IT-Sicherheit – Pflichten und Risiken, Berlin 2005.

---

[69]   Cf. Cauers/Haas/Jakob/Kremer/Schartmann/Welp (2008), p. 2718 f.

Böhm: IT-Compliance als Triebkraft von Leistungssteigerung und Wertbeitrag der IT, in: Handbuch der Wirtschaftsinformatik 263/2008, p. 15–29.

Burch: Auditing for Compliance, in: Internal Auditor December 2008, p. 53–59.

Broadbent/Kitzis: The new CIO Leader. Setting the Agenda and Delivering Results, Boston 2005.

Cauers/Haas/Jakob/Kremer/Schartmann/Welp: Ist der gegenwärtig viel diskutierte Begriff „Compliance" nur alter Wein in neuen Schläuchen?, in: Der Betrieb 50/2008, p. 2717–2719.

Damke: Corporate Governance in mittelständischen Kapitalgesellschaften – Bedeutung der Business Judgement Rule und der D&O-Versicherung für Manager im Mittelstand nach der Novellierung des § 93 AktG durch das UMAG, Edewecht 2007.

Regierungskommission Deutscher Corporate Governance Kodex (DCGK):German Corporate Governance Code, version dated 14 June 2007, www.corporate-governance-code.de/ger/download/D_Kodex %202007_final.pdf,accessed on 30 October 2008.

Dietrich/Schirra: IT im Unternehmen. Leistungssteigerung bei sinkenden Budgets – Erfolgsbeispiele aus der Praxis, Heideberg 2004.

Funk/Rossmanith/Alber: Corporate Governance in Deutschland. Rasche Entwicklung und hohe Regelungsdichte, in: Der Schweizer Treuhänder 9/2006, p. 657–662.

Heier/Maistry: Wertbeitrag von IT-Governance-Applikationen, in: Praxis der Wirtschaftsinformatik 264, p. 93–103.

Hoffmann-Riem: Rechtswissenschaftliche Innovationsforschung als Reaktion auf gesellschaftlichen Innovationsbedarf, verfügbar unter: http://www2.jura.uni-hamburg.de/ceri/publ/download01.pdf, accessed on 19 December 2008.

Homann: Verwaltungscontrolling, Wiesbaden 2005.

Jetter: Produktplanung im Fuzzy Front End. Handlungsunterstützungssysteme auf der Basis von Fuzzy Cognitive Maps, Wiesbaden 2004.

Kaiser: Wirtschaftsprüfung und Fraud-Prävention, 30th Work Congress Taxes and Audit of Professors at Universities of Applied Science from 28 – 30 April 2008, lecture held on 29 April 2008.

Klotz/Dorn: IT-Compliance – Begriff, Umfang und relevante Regelwerke, in: Handbuch der Wirtschaftsinformatik 263/2008, p. 5 –14.

Lensdorf/Steger: IT-Compliance im Unternehmen, in: Der IT-Rechts-Berater 9/2006, p. 206–210.

Lösler: Das moderne Verständnis von Compliance im Finanzmarktrecht, in: Neue Zeitschrift für Gesellschaftsrecht 3/2005, p. 104 – 108.

Männer: Regulatory Push/Pull als Quelle für Innovationen – Konzeptionalisierung und Institutionalisierung, doctorate thesis at the Law and Economics Faculty of the Friedrich-AlexanderUniversity Erlangen-Nuremberg, Nuremberg 2007.

Marbacher: Risikoorientierte Prüfung – ein Muss, in: Der Schweizer Treuhänder 11/2000, p. 1179–1184.

Meyer: Ethikrichtlinien internationaler Unternehmen und deutsches Arbeitsrecht, in: Neue Juristische Wochenzeitschrift 50/ 2006, p. 3601–3607.

Philipp: Software-Zertifizierung nach IDW PS 880, in: Proceedings 3rd Conference on Quality Engineering in Software Technology and VDE-ITG Workshop on Testing Non-Functional Software-Requirements (CONQUEST '99) Nuremberg, 27–29 September 1999, p. 154–162.

Rosinus: Grenzen und Ansatzpunkte einer globalen Compliance-Organisation, in: Zeitschrift für Risk, Fraud und Governance 6/2008, p. 260–266.

Ruud/Isufi/Friebe: Pflicht zur Prüfung der Existenz des Internen Kontrollsystems, Bestandsaufnahme zur Steuerung und Kontrolle mittelgroßer Unternehmen in der Schweiz, in: Der Schweizer Treuhänder 11/2008, p. 938–942.

Schneider: Compliance als Aufgabe der Unternehmensleitung, in: Zeitschrift für Wirtschaftsrecht 15/2003, p. 645–650. Teubner/Feller: Informationstechnologie, Governance und Compliance, in: Wirtschaftsinformatik 5/2008, p. 400–407.Theusinger/Liese: Rechtliche Risiken der Corporate Governance-Erklärung, in: Der Betrieb 26/2008, p. 1419–1423.

UMICert: Compliance nicht nur im Datenschutz durch zertifiziertes IT-Sicherheitszertifikat, in: Der Betrieb 17/2007, p. 877.

von Hehn/Hartung: Unabhängige interne Untersuchungen in Unternehmen als Instrument guter Corporate Governance – auch in Europa?, in: Der Betrieb 36/2006, p. 1909–1914.

Weimar/Grote: Rechtsaudit im Unternehmen – Perspektiven und Chan cen eines innovativen Consultingbereichs, in: Wirtschaftsrechtliche Beratung 16/1997, p. 841–847.

Ziegleder: Corporate Governance of Security, in: Monatsschrift für Kriminologie und Strafrechtsreform 2–3/2007, p. 243–249.

Continuous Auditing: Myth and Reality

By Adrian Garrido[70]

Continuous Auditing is not a new concept; back in 1987 the Treadway Report high-lighted the benefits of using technology to monitor financial transactions on a continuous basis. It appears that this idea has been the future of our function for over twenty years, though it is not clear when it will form part of the present.

Summary 1: Although Continuous Auditing is a powerful concept, it is key to understand its limits and difficulties. Let's be realistic, simple and flexible.

Summary 2: Continuous Audit projects are not all about technology; human judgement and manual procedures are as least as important. No methodology or system can replace a qualified auditor.

1   Great Promises

Continuous Auditing is, without any doubt, one of the most fashionable terms in our profession. As a proof, it is enough to see the use and misuse of this word in any kind of articles, software vendors or consultant brochures, and professional forums, all of them making promises about quantum leaps in the efficiency and effectiveness of the function through tools capable of monitoring all the processes of a company, as well as identifying the appearance of new risks in real time.

Are we in front of the Philosopher's Stone of Internal Auditing? Is this the tool which will definitely allow us to materialize and demonstrate the added value of our function in a conclusive way? From a practical point of view, this article "one more about this issue" is a reflection on this concept but taking into account that our companies demand great ideas and revolutionary conceptual models not being just appearance but having real results in management improvements.

Continuous Auditing has traditionally been defined as the set of automated methods used for performing audit activities on a more frequent basis. This definition is

---

[70]   Adrián Garrido (CIA) is Head of Internal Audit – South America Region at BBVA Group (agarridoh@grupobbva.com)

based around two central principles: the technology and the on-line view of the risks. The combination of these two principles results in the following advantages:

- Detection of new risks and problems as they occur, which means ultimately overcoming the old concept of audit cycle, usually measured in years.
- Efficiency, greater coverage of risks with less effort and as additional benefit less traveling expenses.
- A deeper and wider scope. The use of technology would allow us to have a global view of our companies and at the same time to be capable of easily reaching the greatest level of detail, the transaction. Thus, the problem of defining samples disappears. Why select a group of transactions when it is possible to perform tests on the whole universe?

2   …Not Always Fulfilled

The theoretical advantages offered by the concept are clear and they fit in perfectly with the growing demands of our times: a much more agile, quick and efficient audit function. Nevertheless and once we have reviewed all these positive aspects, it is necessary to come back to reality and to bring forth some additional considerations:

- First, this is not a modern term: back in 1987 the Treadway report highlighted the advantages of using technology to perform a continuous supervision of financial transactions. It would therefore appear that the concept of Continuous Auditing has represented the future of our function for over twenty years though it is not clear when it will form part of the present.
- Secondly, there is much confusion about the real meaning of Continuous Auditing, terms like Continuous Monitoring, Continuous Assurance or Continuous Risks Assessment are interconnected and mixed, raising doubts as to where the separation lies between management's responsibility and that of Audit:
  - Is monitoring operations in real time a control task that should be performed by the line or could this be an Audit function?
  - Should it not rather be the Audit's task to perform a continuous supervision of the controls applied by the line?
  - Should the Continuous Auditing be centered in the continuous assessment of risk?
  - In fact, what is exactly the meaning of "continuous"? Are we talking about real-time, daily or monthly activities?
- Finally and most important, despite all that has been written and the many theoretical advantages, it appears that, according to a recent statement of Richard Chambers, president of the IIA, no one has yet been able to put a truly global Continuous Auditing model into practice.

These practical and theoretical difficulties surrounding the concept have been widely debated and discussed in countless documents. A recent article from CFO.com under the title of "Internal Audit the continuous conundrum" began by stating that: "... A generally accepted definition of Continuous Auditing remains elusive, and expert practitioners remain rare".

This article do not intend to resolve these questions since there is not an easy answer and, above all, because they depend on the specific circumstances of each company. But, beyond theoretical discussions, practical experience can help us to identify guidelines and initiatives that can work and which can be distinguished from those with questionable results.

3   Easier Said than Done

The above reflections give rise to the following question: If the benefits of Continuous Auditing are so evident, then why has its development been so slow? As it happens with so many theoretical models, the answer lies in the difficulty for implementation. In short, our companies are too big and complex to think that it is possible actually to have a real-time control over what is happening in every area and even less so at a transactional level.

These are some of the difficulties we can find when taking on Continuous Auditing projects in the real world:

–   In the first place, in many cases the company systems are not integrated enough, so the development of a Continuous Auditing project becomes a nightmare of interfaces which additionally have to be reprogrammed every time that there are modifications in the source applications.
–   The rhythm of change in our companies is so fast (new products, markets or systems) that a project to monitor a business or a specific process runs the risk of becoming irrelevant even before having ended because the risks intended to be covered have changed.
–   Moreover, the problems and complexities that are inherent to any systems development are also present in this kind of projects, with perhaps an added difficulty for justifying a relevant investment in resources for something that does not have a particularly clear and tangible return.

4   Developments up to Now

Despite the aforementioned difficulties, it is true that there are some examples of companies in the market which have successfully applied Continuous Auditing techniques in different fields. In various publications, firms such as Microsoft,

McDonalds, HP, HCA or Wells Fargo have explained the models implemented and the apparently satisfactory results obtained.

BBVA's Internal Audit has been applying Continuous Auditing techniques for many years within the Branch Network and currently there is a considerably mature model that follows two lines of work:

– A Risk Assessment Module which receives information on a monthly basis regarding risk factors (operational and credit) that are related to branches and customers. Through a scoring system, a ranking is established making possible to select the branches which will be reviewed through physical audits, as well as the customers whose credit risk will be remotely analyze by means of another specific module.
– A system of daily Alerts related to credit, operational, fraud and compliance risks. These alerts are investigated by a specialized team that interacts on-line with the branches in order to request supporting documentation and to clarify the reasons for the root of the alert. The objective of this system is to identify specific problems as well as to produce a control environment.

The following characteristics can be identified in these experiences: the existence of important economies of scale, a careful selection of the indicators to be supervised, a constant feedback and adjustment of those indicators and finally the design of clear procedures for communication and resolution of problems.

5 Five Dangerous Ideas

But even for those organizations that have made any progress in this kind of projects, the next challenge is how to extend the focus on Continuous Auditing to other risks and areas. Is this possible or this approaches should be left only for certain processes or activities?

To answer this question I have identified five "false friends" in referring to ideas which appear very appealing at a theoretical level but can lead us down high risk paths if they are not properly focused:

1. **Focusing on a transactional level.** In addition to the risks linked to the aforementioned problem in implementing Continuous Auditing models, two more can be added:

   – First, at some point in the future the management could consider that the monitor responsibility is theirs and not that of Audit.

   –   Secondly, an excessive focus on operations could cause us to lose sight of the overall picture, where the most important risks generally lie.

2. **The "Large" Continuous Auditing System**. Developing an application with excessively global aspirations can be very risky. It is preferable to use more flexible approaches and set more specific objectives. In many cases, the most efficient alternative is to directly use the functionalities that already are included by the company's transactional systems.

3. **Real-Time Auditing**. This is not a realistic objective except for very punctual areas. The audit cycle approach will still continue being valid for some time and the target would rather be that of obtaining shorter cycles that are more flexible and have a greater focus on risk.

4. **Continuous Auditing is entirely based on Technology.** This is not always the case. The required effort for automating data capture and analysis is often excessive with relation to the result and the most important information is often found in manual formats that cannot be easily automated (Word, PowerPoint, Excel).

5. **The demise of Traditional Auditing.** In my opinion Continuous Auditing will not replace the traditional mode. Instead, it is necessary to integrate both concepts into a new model which combines the best of them.

6   A Practical Proposal

To conclude, I would like to propose an alternative approach and identify possible areas for future advances always taking into account the limitations that have already been highlighted throughout this article.

This approach tries to be simple and pragmatic. Although it perfectly fits with the intensive use of technology, it tries to place technology at the service of the auditor's judgment instead of the contrary, because, as we all know, no methodology or system can replace an auditor with the appropriate degree of expertise, capacity and imagination.

The stages of the process involve:

1. Obtaining relevant information
2. Structured storage of the data
3. A (mainly) qualitative assessment and selection of "focal points"

6.1 Obtaining Relevant Information

We all know that in order to understand a business and to perform good audits, the first thing we need is adequate information. However, the clue does not consist in managing a great deal of information, but in selecting what is truly relevant.

And what is, to a great extent, the most relevant information for a business? The minutes of the Management Committees, Regulatory reports, Management Information, presentations of new projects, new in the press, the minutes of our meetings with the various business areas..., that is the information which has been prepared in universal formats (Word, Excel, PowerPoint) and which can be made available to us without complex and costly interfaces.

The challenge within this stage is to identify such information and to obtain it in a continuous flow and not concentrated at a given moment of the year. This requires very solid communication channels with the rest of the organization.

6.2 Structured Storage of the Data

The second stage is to store this data in a form that is consistent with the structure that we have decided for our Audit Universe. For example, if it is structured based on a classification of Business Units and Processes, we will need a "Filing Cabinet" which allows us to easily store and retrieve relevant information for each of these units.

Once again, we are not speaking of complex applications; but rather of a documentary management system that chronologically organizes the relevant documents, which have been previously identified, and facilitates the preparation of summarized information

6.3 A (mainly) Qualitative Assessment of the Risks and Selection of the "Focal Points"

The next stage is a Risk Assessment process (another, of course, fashionable term) based on the above information, in such a manner that, each time new data is stored, there is an assessment to know to what extend this data implies the appearance of new priorities or risks.

In many cases, the methodologies for Risk Assessment involve numeric models or scoring which assign weightings and scores to different variables with the objective of obtaining a final score for each unit and creating a ranking by risk level.

Although these kinds of models work well for certain types of very homogeneous auditable universes, the model to which we are referring and which is currently being used in BBVA, is mainly a qualitative one based on the auditor's judgment, besides the numerical analysis that would be necessary to provide backing for such judgment.

The main result of this model does not lie so much in a ranking but in the identification of "focal points" or aspects that require special attention in every auditable unit. These focal points can be linked, for example, to:

– Relevant changes in the Business Strategy, Regulations, Systems, etc.
– Areas or processes with weaknesses that have been identified by Audit, by Regulators, or other Control Areas.
– Products or businesses experiencing a high growth.

The identification of these focal points requires a deeper knowledge of the businesses and processes and the simultaneous application of top-down approaches (starting from an overall view of the entity's strategy) and bottom-up approaches (identifying, from the detailed processes, the risks which could have relevant impacts).

Obviously, the identification of these types of aspects as risk areas to be considered within an Audit Plan is not something new. But, the truly relevant fact is the systematic approach to the data used for performing this analysis and the execution of this process on a recurrent basis.

6.4 A Flexible Plan for Audit Activities

Finally, it is necessary to prepare a sufficiently flexible work plan that can be adapted to the focal points identified in the Risk Assessment.

Prior to that, there is a relatively common idea whose validity should be reconsidered: when we prepare an Audit Plan, we normally think in terms of "projects"; in other words, audits for which a team executes some stages in a well defined order: planning, fieldwork, discussion of action plans, issuance of the report and follow up of recommendations.

There are, nevertheless, other types of audit activities whose effectiveness and efficiency can be far superior to that of a classical Project, and which should be included in the Plan with the same status and level of importance, for example:

– Periodic analysis of management information
– Periodic or specific meetings with Management
– Focused reviews of Data Bases using audit tools such as ACL or IDEA

The combination of this type of activities with traditional reviews allows us to have a much richer and adaptable "toolbox" for preparing the Plan. If we compare this to a Lego, we would be managing pieces of different size and utility which can be assembled and unassembled with greater ease depending on the objective in mind.

With these elements, the final phase consists of periodical (for example, quarterly) revisions of the Plan and making the corresponding changes. This does not mean, however, throwing away the concept of Annual Plan, but to adjust it and adapt it to new priorities.

Managing a Plan with this degree of flexibility undoubtedly presents important challenges, ranging from the pure logistics of teams to the culture itself of the people involved. The auditor is no longer responsible for performing a list of predetermined tasks but he/she becomes responsible for monitoring businesses and activities, identifying risks and, in each case, performing those activities that are best adapted to the risks identified.

7   Back to Basis

As a conclusion, since it couldn't be in any other way, the fundamental component for any Continuous Auditing approach (or for any Audit approach) continues to be, over and above technology, the auditor as such. An auditor with an ever changing and demanding profile, willing to assume new challenges with flexibility and imagination, and capable of understanding in great detail the business, maintaining a fluid line of communication with Management and using technology in an intelligent manner.

Internal Audit
in the Economic Crisis

The Financial Sector: Risks, Controls and Assurance after the Financial Crisis[71]

By Daniel Nelson – International Monetary Fund

From Summer 2007, when the early signs of the crisis were observed, until April 2009, broad global mark-to-market potential estimated losses – including the US, Euro-area, Japan, and the UK – grew up to USD 4.1 trillion or 7 percent on a total stock of USD 57.7 trillion. How was it possible to fall into the deepest global economic downturn since the 1930s?

Providing a complete answer obviously is an extremely complex task, but we can roughly summarise four main kinds of causes: macroeconomic, meaning big-picture economics issues; market discipline failures; inadequate market policies and risk management failures.

1   The Roots of the Crisis

The macroeconomic aspects tell us the financial crisis was preceded by the culmination of a long-lasting boom in good credit conditions, combined or feeding into an increased appetite for risks and for leveraging. All of this was accompanied by a rapid increase in complex structured financial products. The situation has been described as presenting the classic preconditions of a massive financial crisis: trillions of dollars of debt, secured by an asset bubble just waiting to pop. Unfortunately this is a hindsight analysis.

The market discipline failures were represented by the increase of improper incentives in underwriting, and packaging and rating debt instruments. This category of underlying causes also includes compensation packages directed at short term gains at the expense of longer term growth and stability. Banks set up numerous off-balance sheet entities to facilitate rapid growth and to generate fee incomes: when the crisis started unfolding the risks or responsibility for these off-balance sheet entities came starkly back. We today know investors' search for yield undermined their due diligence.

---

[71]   The contents of this article represent only the personal views of the author and nothing here should be attributed to the IMF, its Executive Board, or its management.

For what concerns the underlying policies causes, three examples can be made. Basically, the regulatory and supervisory oversight norms—nationally and internationally—lagged behind the rapid innovation and changes taking place in the market. Another area is central bank liquidity frameworks: when the sudden liquidity crunch struck at the start of the financial crisis, many central banks' liquidity frameworks or how they can inject money into the markets could not be flexible enough. Third, the rules on valuation, disclosure, and accounting appear also to have exacerbated the situation.

Lastly, risk management. One aspect is that risk management or risk mitigation has been viewed as more of a nuisance, more a need to adhere to compliance requirements, rather than a useful and integrated part of the business. Most risk units in fact were also placed in a support function role for the most part, not integrated with the business lines. Risk-assessments were excessively model-driven, with less reliance on historical data and even a lesser reliance on longer-term historical data.

2   Key Lessons-learned

On a general level, one of the key lessons-learned from the financial crisis was the need for better coordination among the major economies. As a consequence, one of the first steps was to increase the meetings among countries and economics authorities that could do that, with a prominent role of the G-20. Since November 2008, the G-20 has held its meetings with the countries being represented by their respective heads of state or government. It had never done that before the financial crisis, when only ministers and central bankers would attend, not the heads of state or government, so there is definitely more clout at the table now.

Through the G-20 a series of steps have been put in place. First, as immediate reaction to the crisis, three main directions were followed: fiscal policy interventions by the countries; an increase to the funding resources of the IMF; and central banks' monetary interventions, aimed at increasing liquidity and finding ways to get credit flowing to businesses again. Second step was the effort by G-20 to coordinate the international response to the crisis, through further reform and strengthening of the IMF, review and reform of banking regulations –particularly seeking to cover cross-border cooperation and coordination– and increased international supervision. Third, the coordination of the so-called exit strategies, which essentially means that the governments and the public sector would gradually take steps to reduce or eliminate the financial assistance and guarantee programs put in place initially through the fiscal stimulus programs.

3   Learning from Errors

Turning to a more specific level, what have internal auditors learned and what can be done differently looking forward?

An example can give us an opportunity to delineate some important themes in the perspective of the world of internal audit: the AIG's near collapse, and salvation by the US government.

In extreme summary, AIG had entered into a line of business based on financial derivatives, especially on credit-default swaps (CDSs) that are lightly-regulated insurance-like contracts used to protect investors against the default or loss in market value of a security. CDSs protect assets – the most common of these protected assets were collateralized-debt obligations or CDOs, which are groupings of mortgages or other debt that are divided up and sliced into tranches, each of which has a different risk and return profile. The business model used by AIG was reportedly based on the principle that if the swaps activity, the CDSs, was backed by a financially strong company, like one with a rating of AAA, that would give a lot of competitive advantage to operate in the markets and keep financing costs low.

That financially strong company was AIG, and one of the major players in CDSs was AIG Financial Products (AIGFP) which AIG took over in the early 1990s. The higher the credit rating, the lower the collateral obligations, meaning AIGFP did not have to put up as much capital for its operations as would have been the case with a lower credit rating.

On September 16, 2008 AIG lost its AA- rating (it had already lost its AAA rating in 2005), and that triggered its trading partners to suddenly ask AIG for billions of dollars more in collateral—but AIG didn't have the money. On September 16, the Federal Reserve extended an USD 85 billion credit to AIG in exchange for about 80 % of the ownership of the company.

Leaving apart the technical causes of the collapse and the way CDSs and CDOs were administered in AIG, let's look at a few areas that appear relevant to internal audit.

4   Lessons for Internal Auditors

First of all it has been reported that internal audit did not have sufficient or adequate access to AIGFP. Assuming that this was the case, the first elementary lesson-learned is that internal audit should have adequate and complete audit scope coverage of areas with important risks. The second observation would be that internal audit should not have any restriction in terms of access to review any area in an entity.

It has also been reported that enterprise risk management (ERM) and the finance complex did not have adequate oversight or coverage of the AIGFP business, particularly on AIGFP's valuation practices, its risk models. According to public records, this appears to have been a major concern also for the external auditor. Other reports indicate that risk taking at AIGFP had deteriorated particularly in the last few years before the collapse—the exposure increased significantly, and the quality of the swaps was low because they were mostly unhedged. The lesson-learned here is obvious: internal audit should review the risk management governance and operational arrangements, to ensure that there are no such gaps. The completeness of the checks and balances set up by the finance complex should also be reviewed.

A third major weakness reported was the lack of clarity over internal control rules and responsibilities for the organization as a whole and the fourth one was the role of the audit committee. For the latter, in my research I found no specific information on weaknesses other than a suggestion that the committee was not as much involved perhaps in the review and oversight of the work of internal audit, when its charter is compared to charters in other financial institutions. But when I went to look at their charter, I found two interesting changes between the 2006 charter and the 2009 charter. The first change is the introduction in the 2009 charter of specific wording to indicate that the committee will review and approve internal audit's annual work plan and its financial budget; this is a new requirement compared to the 2006 charter. The second change in the 2009 charter is the new wording added to the risk management section which indicates that the audit committee is not the only body responsible for oversight of AIG's risk assessment and management. The 2009 charter also goes on to state that AIG manages and assesses its risk through multiple mechanisms other than the oversight of the audit committee, including the oversight of other committees of the Board. I submit that these key changes are important lessons-learned, and that they tie-in to the weaknesses in internal audit and in risk management.

5   Four more steps
In closing, I want to suggest the following four specific areas to be considered for audit work by internal audit.

As mentioned, risk management will certainly be an area to focus internal audit's attention on; admittedly, the current crisis involved both external risks and systemic risks that impacted many of our organizations and these types of risks are even more difficult to identify and assess. The financial crisis in any event has taught us that we should also consider velocity, preparedness, and resilience, when assessing risk impact and probability.

The next area can be called a "back to basics" direction for internal audit: cost reductions and costs savings. A form of zero-based review could be considered, where internal audit can review from the bottom up every activity that is necessary or where savings may be achieved if the resources are not being applied in line with the mandate of the unit, and in line with the mandate and the priorities of the organization. Some might say that "back to basics" should also include an increased emphasis on testing and focus on fraud weaknesses that may have been exacerbated by the recession. Information systems security, an area to keep in focus in any event, also comes to mind.

Moving forward, in many countries there has already been an increase in regulatory compliance work. In addition, for those entities that have received public funds we can all assume that those resources will be closely scrutinized, particularly in the public media. I submit as discussed earlier that it is likely that financial regulations and regulators may further increase, in other areas, in other countries and among countries. In that case, internal audit would have greater involvement in conducting preparatory compliance reviews.

Last but again certainly not least, regulatory compliance leads me to discuss executive compensation. There is another perspective aside from compliance with possible salary caps and other conditions imposed by the fact of receiving public funds. We discussed earlier that the misalignment between risk management and compensation policies was also seen as one of the factors contributing to this financial crisis. It would be interesting for internal audit to review whether the organization's compensation policies and model are indeed appropriately tailored to its business model or whether it is a risk in itself.

Doing More with Less

By Neil Baker

In the current economic crisis, how can internal auditors deliver value and assurance with fewer resources?

Geoffrey Storms is philosophical about the impact of the economic downturn on his internal audit function. His current employer recruited him four years ago to build an audit function from scratch. His team has been working hard to educate management and the board about what internal audit does, and why it is important. He's been making real progress. So how does he feel now that his budget is being cut? "If I was a newly minted auditor, I would probably be angry," he says. "But I've been in the profession for a long time, and I've experienced this kind of downsizing in other organisations. If I know in advance that I'm going to be somewhat resource constrained, then I can deal with it."

Despite the stoicism, Storms says he argued against the budget cuts. He told senior management at the mining company where he is the head of internal audit that pruning audit resources in a downturn is not a prudent course of action. Why not? "Because in times of belttightening, organisations often face greater risks. It's not a time to start losing controls; it might even be a time to strengthen them," he says. Storms is not alone. Other internal auditors have been waging the same battle, trying to persuade people who hold the corporate purse strings that now would be the worst time to cut audit resources. Naturally, the heads of other corporate functions are making the same argument about their respective services. When times are tough, every corporate function will fight to protect its piece of a shrinking budget pie. So does internal audit really deserve special protection? And if it does have to take a share of the pain – which seems to be the case for most audit functions – how can heads of internal audit rework their plans so they continue to deliver assurance and value with less money?

1   Budget Crunch

Storms met his budget cut by losing two front-line audit posts. His internal audit team has three managers, each with his or her own audit staff – there were 15 people in total, nine of whom actually worked on audits. That number has fallen to seven.

"We examined the audit plan for 2009 and considered how we would accomplish our objectives with two fewer staff members," Storms says. They eventually determined that a different approach was necessary:

The plan had to change, and some of the audits had to be eliminated. Storms discussed the issue with his audit committee. When he joined the company four years ago, the committee gave him a mandate to identify and risk-rate its audit universe, and then audit all the high-risk areas within five years. "This downsizing puts us at risk of not being able to do that," he says. Storms conveyed this message to management and the board, but to little avail. "They understand, but they are prepared to live with some of the risks," he adds.

One way of covering the same audit plan while cutting costs would be to reduce the time spent on each audit. Storms ruled out that option. These were mostly first-time audits; a great deal of uncertainty existed around the level of inherent risk in some business areas, in addition to residual risk, he explains. He told the audit committee that performing fewer audits was better than cutting quality. How did the committee respond? "I'll put it this way: It wasn't a brief conversation," he says.

2   Show the Impact

The key to convincing an audit committee that less internal audit budget equates to less assurance is to be specific about the work internal audit can no longer perform, says Richard Chambers, president of the global IIA. He advises showing committee members the audit plan and specifically identifying the audits that will be removed. That gives the audit committee the chance to request that some audits stay on the plan, and that others are cut instead. "The head of internal audit's conversation with the audit committee needs to be tangible and real in terms of the impact on audit coverage," Chambers says. "Otherwise surprises inevitably will surface later." Talk vaguely about a reduction in audit coverage, and individual audit committee members might develop different ideas about what the audit function is likely to cut, he warns.

The head of internal audit should ask the committee what areas it wants to prioritise, he says. "It's easy for chief audit executives to start by identifying audits that their department needs to keep doing, but they should first talk to stakeholders and obtain their assessment of where the audit department should focus. Ask them: 'What should we be doing for you?'" Reigning in expectations in this way is important, Chambers says. In many instances, auditors mistakenly believe they have to maintain the same audit coverage from the previous year, but with fewer people. However, that approach will impact quality, he warns.

If the audit committee insists that the audit plan stays the same, Chambers recommends that heads of internal audit review the scope of each assignment – just like they would the entire audit plan – and focus on the high-risk areas that offer the greatest value for resources expended. "Any audit function taking that approach must be fully transparent in its audit reports about the level of coverage and about any objectives or risks that were not addressed because of budget constraints," he says. "That will make the report more useful and valuable and prevent the reader from misinterpreting the level of coverage internal audit has provided."

Determining how to redirect audit efforts can involve a difficult balancing act. For example, heads of internal audit often report to two masters: the finance chief, who sets the audit budget, and the audit committee, which receives the assurance that this budget pays for. What if the audit committee wants the same level of assurance but the finance department wants to cut the budget? "If the chief financial officer has decided that the audit function should be reduced, it is vital for the audit committee to be aware of that," Chambers says. And if the committee members don't know about it, internal audit should tell them, he adds. "I would never advocate that internal auditors play one of their stakeholders against the other, but they do have a responsibility to make sure the audit committee is aware of any resource issues or challenges they face."

3   Changing Risk Profile

Budget cuts are not the only reason to revisit the audit plan in a downturn: The risk profile of the organisation is likely to be changing too. A recent survey from The IIA's Global Audit Information Network – Knowledge Report: 2009 Hot Topics for the Internal Audit Profession – showed how auditors around the world are refocusing their audit efforts to reflect a changing economic climate. A third of organisations in the survey say the downturn is affecting the focus of their work, with the risk of fraud representing the main area receiving extra attention. Half of the respondents feel that budget cuts across their organisation would damage its control environment and its ability to achieve business outcomes this year. The survey said auditors should be reviewing what the organisation is doing to maintain its control coverage, but the majority (58 %) have no plans to do any work on this risk.

Jim LaTorre is managing partner of PricewaterhouseCoopers' U.S. internal audit practice and the head of internal audit at a large hospitality and leisure company. He says internal auditors need to look at what they do from a wider perspective. "There are ways to fight this problem and still maintain a degree of cost effectiveness," he says, "but it's going to require knocking down some of the old barriers and revisiting established thinking to find a solution that works best for the organisation." For example, internal auditors need to focus more on the risks that could destroy shareholder value, or stop the organisation from building value, LaTorre says. For some, that would entail a significant re-examination of internal audit's role in relation to risk.

Michael Fucilli, auditor general at the Metropolitan Transportation Authority in New York City, is one of the heads of internal audit who has been changing his audit focus. His team is doing more work on procurement fraud; for example, trying to spot fraudsters who submit fictional invoices in the hope they'll be paid. It is also checking the way contracts are awarded, looking at background checks on suppliers, and auditing payroll. "Believe it or not, I even added petty cash audit to the plan this year," Fucilli says. With the organisation's high-risk areas so well controlled, trouble can arise in the seemingly low-risk areas, he reasons. "I've added more audit coverage to some of my low-risk areas, just to make sure that they really are low."

Chambers' advice to heads of internal audit: "Perform an end-to-end examination of your audit processes." Inefficiencies in audit execution often result from too much documentation, he says, and too little use of technology. The three key processes are planning, fieldwork, and reporting, he says, and auditors should review all of them. When Chambers was head of the US Army's Global Internal Review and Audit Compliance Department in the early 1990s his team created what they called the Quick Response Audit. "It was specifically tailored to get audit results out quickly and to minimise the impact on the number of audits we could generate. It proved to be a popular concept with our stakeholders, because they realised we were focusing on the most critical issues and getting them answers in a much more timely fashion."

4   Avoid the Cut

How can audit functions that have budgets still intact avoid the CFO 's knife? "I wouldn't wait for senior management to come to me and say, 'We are all contributing toward cost cuts: It's your turn,'" LaTorre says. Fucilli agrees. "Be proactive," he says. "You can't sit back and wait for the company to come to you. You have to identify key issues in the organisation and speak with appropriate personnel. Don't say, 'how can I help you?' say 'I know how I can help you – here's how.' I'd say nine times out of 10 they will take up the offer."

Fucilli has been looking for tangible ways to help business managers. He's been meeting with them, attending their staff meetings, and inquiring about the issues they face. Spending time with managers led to a recent assignment on medical costs. "People say that some items are simply runaway costs that cannot be controlled. I've been to meetings and heard people say we couldn't control medical costs. Of course we can!" he says. "We audited them and saved USD 5.5 million, and the company received a cheque back from our insurer. That gets people's attention."

Fucilli sums up his approach: "We are not in the audit report business; we are not even in the audit recommendation business. Instead, we are in the change business – how to address risk and how to make the company better. It's not easy to audit this way, but if you search out areas where you can help, then your audit business will boom and they will not cut your department."

Fucilli's audit function has become a profit centre, because of the cost savings it finds. The team of 100 auditors completes 175 audits a year across a universe of 561 activities. Last year it saved the organisation USD 61m, against a budget for the function of USD 15m. Even so, Fucilli has been told to make a 5 % saving. But that's a lot less than other departments in his organisation have been told to save. He met the target by automating more of his processes. And his head count has actually increased, because nine auditors who specialise in engineering compliance have been transferred to his team. "Because of the work we do and the assurance we deliver, the audit function is one of the most important departments in the organisation," he says.

For internal auditors, now is not the time to be a corporate wallflower or to disengage from the debate about shifting organisational priorities. Audit leaders should promote their functions' value as never before and redouble their efforts to ensure their work addresses the changing risks facing their organisations.

But what should internal auditors do on a personal level? In tough economic times, people are bound to worry about their career prospects. "My advice to internal auditors who are being impacted by the recession is to take this opportunity to make themselves distinctive in terms of their professional credentials," Chambers says. "They should look at their investment in professional education and training and obtain whatever additional certifications they can. Auditors are more likely to be successful if they can demonstrate the excellence and quality of their work."

The current economic crisis will be deeper than any we have experienced in recent times, Chambers acknowledges. "But I think that internal auditors will survive and persevere, and the profession will come out strong and effective on the other side." Storms was chief auditor at a large Canadian insurance company when recession last hit in the early 1990s. What lessons did he learn? "First of all, don't panic," he says. "As auditors, we control our own destinies. We can decide what is going to be audited, when it is going to be audited, and what the scope will be. If you've got a mandate, an audit charter, an independent reporting structure, an audit universe, and a plan, then all of the necessary components are in place — all you've got to do is manage your way through it. You've still got control."

An Audit Makeover

In this tough economic climate, internal auditors should think about giving their function a quick four-step makeover:

1. Review your last risk assessment. Everything has changed so dramatically in the last few months that you may be chasing risks that are significantly down the scale now.
2. Look at the way the audit function works. Find ways to reengineer your department and to stratify those items that are "must-haves" and "nice-to-haves," where you can legitimately cut costs.
3. Review the audit function's skills complement. If it doesn't have the skills needed to deal with the issues in the new risk assessment, look for short-term, creative ways to fill those gaps. One solution might be to bring in guest auditors from other departments.
4. Do not go it alone. Remain in direct, constant communication with the audit committee and management so that you understand their view of emerging risks and where your audit effort should be directed.

Based on comments from Jim LaTorre, managing partner of Pricewaterhouse-Coopers' U.S. internal audit practice.

Future of Internal Auditing

Performance Measurement and Controlling of Internal Audit – More Than Just a Measurement Problem

By Dr. Andreas Langer, Andreas Herzig, Prof. Dr. Burkhard Pedell[72]

Internal audit must face the challenge of measuring, documenting and communicating its added value. For this purpose, the customers and functions of internal audit must first be identified. Significant deficits still exist with performance measurement on this basis. The acceptance of quality assessments has not been very well developed so far and the indicators only allow limited statements to be made about the added value of internal audit. Therefore, clear and transparent criteria should be used as a basis for the selection of indicators; relevance, reactivity, controllability and output orientation are suitable as basic criteria. The further development of the performance measurement and controlling of internal audit should be based on a solid scientific foundation.

1 Introduction

Notwithstanding increasing regulatory requirements for functioning and effective internal audit, it is well advised – as well as any other corporate department – to provide evidence that the resources, which it utilises, and the results generated with these are in an economically beneficial proportion to one another. So far, an extensive methodological debate regarding the controlling of internal processes in internal audit has tended to take place in Anglo-Saxon literature. The question regarding which contribution is provided by internal audit to enterprise value and how this can be measured has also been frequently asked, but has not yet been answered very concretely. The debate surrounding this issue and relevant application-oriented approaches has lagged behind the importance of this subject until now. In fact, internal audit can generally quite rightly refer to a significant contribution that it makes to corporate success, because with sufficient resources, it is able to ensure a distinct improvement to the companies' risk position. However, adequately documenting

---

[72] Dr. Andreas Langer is a Manager at Deloitte & Touche GmbH in the Enterprise Risk Management division; Andreas Herzig is a Partner at Deloitte & Touche GmbH in the Enterprise Risk Services division in Germany and heads up the Internal Audit and Controls Assurance divisions; Prof. Dr. Burkhard Pedell is a Full Professor of Management Accounting and Control at the University of Stuttgart and Member of the Scientific Committee of the DIIR.

and communicating this performance has not yet always succeeded convincingly in the past. The requirement for intensive analytical research and a stronger dialogue between theory and practice regarding the subject of performance measurement and controlling are of key importance in this regard. The following article demonstrates the required development and outlines perspectives for performance measurement and controlling of internal audit.

2   Necessity of Planning and Controlling the Target Contribution of Internal Audit

Planning and controlling aim to base the solving of decision problems (cf. Schweitzer (2001), p. 21) and the behaviour of employees on the company's objectives. With this, information is represented by the basis and result of the decision-making process. Internal audit also inevitably encounters business and controlling decisions, if it intends to contribute to the corporate objectives. It requires appropriate information for planning and controlling its target contribution, which portrays its own performance and makes it controllable on this basis.

The conceptual implementation of performance measurement and controlling (also referred to as performance management) has already been debated very extensively in the literature (cf. Gleich (2001), Klingebiel (2001), Ittner et. al. (2003)). In contrast, the debate regarding concrete concepts for performance measurement and controlling, which is adapted to the service performed by internal audit, has only taken place to a very minor extent so far (this conclusion is also reached by Hölscher/ Rosenthal (2007), p. 42 and Likierman (2006), p. 20 et seqq.). Not least, due to this fact, a study conducted by Kinney et al. concluded that: "Surprisingly, only a few survey participants have yet to formally implement performance metrics linking audit objectives with outcomes (Kinney et al. (2003), p. 13)."

With many services performed by internal audit (also within the context of the corporate governance debate), a transition to monetary indicators has not existed so far, alone due to the inability to isolate individual qualitative factors (e.g. the avoidance of risks and their effect on monetary indicators (cf. Buderath/Langer (2007), p. 133). Intelligent communication and marketing of own services become all the more important with this. Even if the measurement of services performed by internal audit is, as frequently emphasised, associated with significant difficulties, adequate measurement and controlling of its performance are essential.

3   Scope of Service and Communication

As in every other department, the question must first be asked regarding the area of responsibility and the scope of service of internal audit. Only after this, can additional systematic considerations take place regarding performance measurement and controlling in the sense of corporate targets. Regarding the service portfolio of internal audit, the DIIR – Deutsches Institut für Interne Revision (German Institute of Internal Auditors) states: "Internal audit performs independent and objective audit ("assurance") and advisory services, which are aimed at creating added value and improving the business processes. It supports the organisation in the achievement of its targets by assessing the effectiveness of risk management, controls and the management and monitoring processes, using a targeted approach, and helps to improve these (Deutsches Institut für Interne Revision e.V. (2005), p. 35)." In addition to traditional controlling functions, these include subjects such as reviewing the risk management systems, advisory services for increasing the efficiency of company processes and supporting the controlling bodies in their manifold functions.

If internal audit is regarded as an internal service provider under marketing aspects, the basic requirement of marketing to know its own customers and products also applies to it (cf. Berry/Parasuraman (1999), p. 87). Therefore, customers and functions must also be identified by internal audit, who will fall into (or could fall into) its service portfolio now and/or in the future. Development trends in the field of activity of internal audit should also be fundamentally identified and used, if possible (cf. Fig. 1). Concepts from marketing, e.g. the ABC/XYZ analysis or the gap analysis could form a possible framework with the structuring of current and future customers/products (cf. managing the services of internal departments, such as controlling Mosiek (2002) and Langer/Munhoz (2005), p. 663 et seqq.). However, these concepts must be adapted to its specific requirements, under consideration of the general conditions within which internal audit performs its service.

Internal Audit capacity

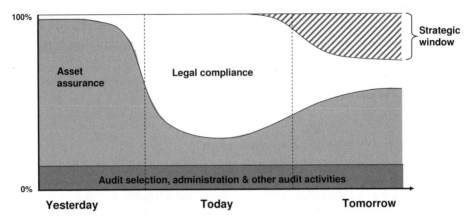

Figure 1: Development trends for internal audit – a forecast (Deloitte & Touche [2008])

When arguing on the basis of the product-market-matrix by Ansoff, the strategic options of market development and diversification are also conceivable for internal audit (for an analogous illustration of the development of controlling cf. Horváth (2008)). However, these require a strong community of interests and an analytical basis, which conceptually advance the range of functions of internal audit. An expandable field of activities is addressed here in an exemplary manner: Internal audit reports directly to the implementing management in a two-tier system and not, for example, to the supervisory boards. Therefore, an effective assessment of upper management and the management processes could be significantly impaired under certain circumstances, due to the balance of power. However, particularly in this position, internal audit could contribute to adding value to the company, e.g. by expanding management audits. The internal audit department will not enforce a change to the company statutes (e.g. an internal audit department that reports to the supervisory board (Audit Committee) in disciplinary and specialist terms) and the balance of power within the company. However, a functioning community of interests could – also on a political level – communicate irregularities to the relevant authority and take advantage of the situation to position the service range of internal audit to enhance value. The resulting advantages for shareholders and other stakeholders would promote this development, if they are then communicated appropriately. Therefore, intelligent communication is just as much a part of successful management of internal audit as the service performance itself.

In addition to communication at a political level, the internal company communication also becomes increasingly important. The interpersonal communication also plays a significant part in the implementation of the audit service. For services such as those also performed by internal audit, the "uno actu principle" generally applies, i.e. for successful performance of services, the involvement of the customer, et al. is required (e.g. management, supervisory bodies or also every audited party). Compliance questions are very complex in many areas. A more detailed review by the audit department, as a service, can be regarded as a means of avoiding criminal charges. The audited parties gain additional security from the review. Therefore, internal audit must position its own services better with management and with the audited parties.

The basis of any successful communication is the verifiably provided performance and therefore also the quality of the service. At this point, quality management in internal audit is therefore addressed.

4 Quality Management and Quality Assessment in Internal Audit

An intensive quality debate regarding internal audit has so far been focussed within the context of the quality assessment. A quality assessment, as such, is conducted every five years (furthermore, the standards prescribe an annual self-assessment) and records the audit performance using a standardised questionnaire (or with a type of checklist). The focus of this is on aspects of organisation and regularity (cf. DIIR – Deutsches Institut für Interne Revision e.V. (2007)). With the type of performance and quality measurement (target contribution measurement) and the subsequent performance communication, the question of positioning arises at the same time. With this, a derivation can be made: If it can be proven, with the fulfilment of the objective intended with the quality assessment, that internal audit functions under "compliance aspects" and if this also already describes the central field of activity of internal audit, then the quality assessment can be regarded as a sufficient approach.

However, if internal audit intends to be more than just an institutionalised "jail prophylaxis" – and this could particularly be linked with the expectations of upper management (cf. Zwingmann (2006)) – then a quality assessment in its current form would not be sufficient for controlling the performance of internal audit in the sense of an extensive added value.

Noteworthy points about the addressed problem are also shown by a panel study by the Institute of Internal Auditors (IIA) (cf. The Institute of Internal Auditors (2007), p. 1 et seqq.). In 2007, most internal auditors (91.7 %) are familiar with the quality standards of IIA (or of the respective national institutes) and the concept of the quality assessments (cf. The Institute of Internal Auditors (2007a), p. 1 et seqq.). However, only 56 % of those surveyed deal with a quality assurance programme and only 34 % deal with the implementation of a quality assessment within their own audit department. When examining the results of the survey in detail, the upper management sees no "value added" in implementing a quality assessment in 14.4 % of the surveyed companies/every fifth company (when deducting the response option of "other reasons"). Another 19 % do not have the time or the budget for this. Only around 37 % are in an active five-year cycle and have therefore not conducted a quality assessment in 2007.

The acceptance with management obviously (still) appears not to be very well-developed. The causes for this could also be sought in the lack of meaningfulness in a quality assessment that is viewed on an isolated basis and in the type of quality measurement. In a similar context, Likiermann also reaches the conclusion: "Measurement needs to be more than asking a few colleagues a few questions ... (Likiermann (2006), p. 24)." (See also Fig. 2.)

What are the main reasons for why a quality assessment has not yet been carried out?			
Answer	Chart	Share	Number of answers
Required budget not available		9.3	82
Insufficient time available		9.9	87
Audit Committee/Management Committee sees no added benefit		14.4	126
Already within the 5-year cycle		37.2	327
Other reasons		29.2	256

Figure 2: Empirical study regarding the quality assessment (cf. The Institute of Internal Auditors (2007), p. 4)

However, control variables can partially be derived from the information that becomes available from the quality assessment, which can flow into a concept for indicators. It is therefore essential for companies and academics to deal more intensively with the subject of performance measurement in internal audit – i.e. with actual performance measurement and control.

5   Performance Measurement in Internal Audit

Within the context of performance measurement, two approaches can basically be pursued: a direct performance measurement and an indirect/relative performance measurement. A relative performance measurement yields an opinion about the performance by comparing the performance of two service units, the selection of which can take place within a company or across companies. However, in the academic world, relative performance measurement is debated very controversially (cf. Hofmann/Daugert (2004), p. 197), as in addition to the level problem (both comparative partners could be below their performance level) as a sole measuring instrument, it also raises the difficulty of adequate comparability between the comparative partners. In internal audit, the field of activity within the companies is also delineated very differently, therefore making a direct performance comparison difficult. Therefore, the relative performance measurement can be regarded as a supplement to performance measurement in the traditional sense, but should not be drawn upon as a sole instrument. This is why a debate regarding the indicators used is essential.

Performance measurement concepts generally combine financial and non-financial indicators into a measurement system. The presumably best-known performance measurement concept is the Balanced Scorecard (cf. Kaplan/Norton (1996)). The challenge with this lies in the systematic and stringent implementation in practice (regarding internal audit, cf. Frigo (2001), p. 31 et seqq.). After all, which and how many indicators should be used for performance measurement in internal audit has only been insufficiently debated so far.

When consulting with the publications that have appeared so far on the subject of performance measurement (mostly from the Anglo-American region), very concrete indicators are usually listed, as shown in Fig. 3 (cf. Frigo (2002), p. 36 et seqq. and Ziegenfuss (2000), p. 40).

When taking a closer look at the indicators mentioned, it is noticeable that the majority of the "performance" indicators used so far are of an input-oriented nature (i.e. no result, but rather, reflects the utilisation of resources). However, other indicators have an output-oriented character, but do not allow any direct statement to be made about the (value) contribution of internal audit (e.g. the indicators, "Number of final reports issued) or "Number of recommended process improvements").

Indicator	Orientation
Number of final reports issued	Output
Average time spent on training	Input
Average degree of experience of the employees	Input
Degree of training of the auditors	Input
Degree of certification of the auditors	Input
Percentage rate of implemented recommendations	Output
Number of recommended process improvements	Output
Satisfaction of management and the Audit Committee	Output
Comparison between planned and implemented audits	Output
Comparison between required time and planned time	Input

Figure 3: Indicators used in internal audit

A study by Blackmore et al. also demonstrates that the majority (57 %) of the indicators used in audit practice portray an extensive target-actual comparison for the fulfilled audit workload – i.e. do not enable a direct statement to be made about the actual (value) contribution of internal audit. According to the study, only approx. 35 % of the indicators used are output-oriented indicators with a clear statement about the added value of internal audit (e.g. customer satisfaction or cost savings from implementation of recommendations by internal audit). Therefore, Likiermann states very clearly "Yet the ways of measuring ... internal audit performance are often surprisingly primitive (Likiermann (2006), p. 20)." (See also Fig. 4.)

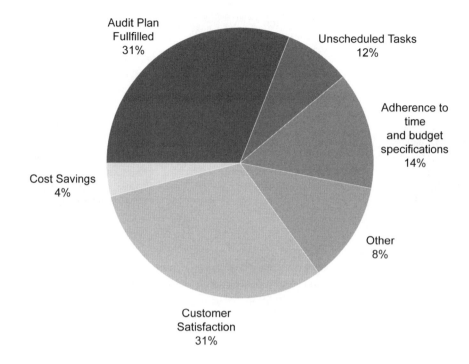

Figure 4: Performance measurement in internal audit (cf. Blackmore, et al. (2004), p. 8)

If internal audit intends to verifiably and perceptibly contribute to the company value/corporate targets, it must record indicators, which portray its contribution to the achievement of corporate targets.

In other departments without direct access to markets, the definition of meaningful performance measurements also confronts the respective department manager with considerable challenges. An extensive, usable definition of suitable indicators or even a prefabricated set of indicators will not be found in internal audit or in any other departments. The tasks are too diverse for this and the structure of the departments – depending on the company – is too different. This allows the following conclusion to be drawn: If an extensive definition of suitable indicators or a set of indicators is not possible, for the purpose of simplification, a process that can be standardised for the determination of indicators could be sought.

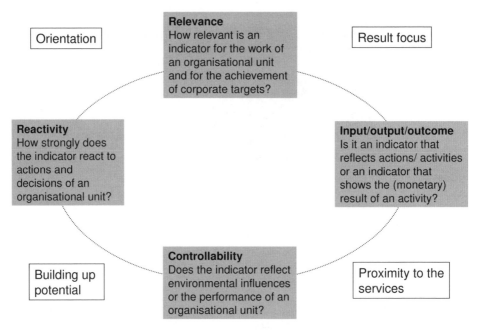

Figure 5: Criteria for indicator assessment

6 A Possible Approach for the Determination of Indicators

As already explained, it is necessary to determine an audit unit's scope for action (performance range) in the individual case. The requirements of the audit customers must be taken into consideration, because: "Each Customer Group has its own value propositions and critical success factors that internal auditing activities must consider in developing performance measures (Frigo (2002), p. 33)."

When the scope for action is determined and the targets from the corporate strategy are broken down onto internal audit, indicators can be discussed within the context of a "workshop" or in a "group analysis", using brainstorming methods. These should fall into the scope of action of internal audit (tasks, customers and corporate targets) and preferably cover it completely. After a phase of gathering key figures, the indicators shall be analysed regarding their suitability for performance measurement. The following principle should generally be adhered to for this: The characteristic of the indicators and not the intuition of the respective manager shall determine the composition of the performance measurement. Systematic prioritisation and selection of indicators are thereby ensured.

The following criteria shall be investigated for the indicator analysis (cf. Langer/Pedell (2010), p. 73 et seqq. and regarding the measurement basis Langer

(2007), p. 104 et seqq. and regarding indicators in the "Audit-Balanced Scorecard" Frigo (2002), p. 31 et seqq.):

6.1 Relevance

Relevance of an indicator can be regarded as the congruence and validity with regard to higher-ranking corporate targets. If an indicator measures a department's contribution to the achievement of corporate targets with high definition (high validity), the indicator has high relevance. This also applies with regard to the contribution of internal audit to the achievement of corporate targets. Therefore, the number of implemented recommendations, which lead to a cost reduction or a decline in corporate risk, should usually have a higher weighting than the number of final reports issued.

6.2 Reactivity

The reactivity of the indicators is also reflected in the "reaction speed" of an indicator. If a direct change takes place to an indicator after the decision and action of a person/department, then the indicator has high reactivity. Indicators with high reactivity therefore show success more quickly and consequently are frequently preferred to be taken into consideration. As the audit services, e.g. within the context of the corporate governance debate, partially have an effect with time lags, performance measures with high reactivity should be chosen. Ideally, performance measures also show very early the expected long term success of a current action.

6.3 Controllability

Environmental influences are disturbance factors (exogenous factors, e.g. management behaviour, quality of external "suppliers" or the corporate culture), on which the audit department has no direct influence. However, if it is only fortune that decides on success or failure, the contribution by internal audit to the corporate targets is no longer measurable. The less effect environmental influences have on an indicator ("signals to noise ratio"), i.e. the more internal audit can influence the respective indicator with its own decisions or the service performed, the more suitable it is for the measurement.

6.4 Input/Output/Outcome Orientation

As already mentioned above, many of the indicators used in internal audit are input-oriented figures. These only measure the use of means to achieve a target (e.g. number of training courses, number of CIAs), but not the result created and therefore the direct contribution to the corporate targets. Output-oriented indicators show the performance of internal audit; however they do not measure it in monetary terms. For the quantification of the value added of internal audit, outcome-oriented indicators are preferable. Input- and output-oriented measures should only be used, when monetary quantification of the performance of internal audit is not possible. (See also Fig. 6).

Test Criteria	Weighting Rule	Scaling	Weight
Relevance	*positive* correlation with the level of relevance	high relevance index value = 10 *to* low relevance index value = 0	[rating result]
Controllability	*positive* correlation with the level of controllability	high controllability index value = 10 *to* low controllability index value = 0	[rating result]
Reactivity	*positive* correlation with the level of reactivity	high reactivity Index value = 10 *to* low reactivity Index value = 0	[rating result]
Input/Output/ Outcome	**outcome** higher weighted than **output** **output** higher weighted than **input**	outcome Index value = 10 output index value = 5 input index value = 0	[rating result]
		Total index for indicator x	Min. 0 Points Max. 40 Points

Figure 6: Assessment and selection of indicators using scoring

In order to calculate the total weighting, i.e. to determine the significance of an indicator on the basis of the criteria that have just been described, a highly simplified scoring model is recommended, the assessment rules for which are shown in Fig. 6 (the scaling can be individually structured in the respective case; the scaling shown in Fig. 6 only represents a possible example). When the indicators gathered within the context of the brainstorming are now drawn upon and assessed on the basis of the four criteria listed above (e.g. within the context of a systematic Delphi analysis (cf. Volkmann (2007))), this results in a total weighting per indicator. This weighting can now be used for the selection of suitable indicators, i.e. the higher the weighting (index value), the more significant the respective indicator is. However, this poses the problem of the number of indicators and the balance within the set of indicators.

In the literature regarding performance measurement, and particularly the Balanced Scorecard, the 'rule of thumb' of 20 indicators is frequently recommended. The trade-off behind the number of indicators is intended to be illustrated with two quotes: "Healthy common sense already suggests that ... organisations ... required a balanced system of key figures ... and that fewer indicators are better than too many" (Brown (1997), p. 6). This can be countered with: "The diversity of operational decisions is to be accounted for with a corresponding diversity of performance measures (Hofmann (2001), p. 96)." Internal audit must therefore decide in each individual case, on the basis of its chosen orientation and fields of activity, which scope of information it requires and is able to process for adequate control of the department.

In order to establish the "balance", e.g. the Balanced Scorecard" classifies the indicators into four perspectives (subjects regarding finance, processes, customers and employees) with an adequate distribution of the indicators per perspective. This classification can also be used within the context of internal audit (cf. Frigo (2002), p. 31 et seqq.), by implementing an indicator enumeration, prioritisation and selection per perspective (with the result of e.g. five selected indicators per perspective).

The advantages of such an approach could be sought in explanation of the indicator selection, as well as a generally usable basis for performance measurement and control of internal audit. Not least, the debate regarding indicators increases the transparency of the services performed and relevant influence factors with all parties involved. Whether the frequently-described cause-effect chains between the selected indicators in the traditional sense (heuristically) need to be established must be decided in the individual case. However, the more the link to outcome-oriented financial key figures, which must not be missed in a set of indicators for internal audit, is implemented, the more internal audit is able to prove a (monetary) quantifiable contribution to the corporate targets.

Measurement, control and communication of the audit services therefore form important strategic fields of activity, for which a great deal of room still exists in internal audit for development possibilities.

7   Conclusion

It can currently be stated that the demand for audit services has increased in recent years and will presumably continue to do so in the future. With this, the control systems for the measurement of audit performance, also based on generally accepted methods and concepts, become all the more important.

The development status regarding performance measurement and control within internal audit continues to lag significantly behind other business disciplines. A fully-developed system/concept has not been identified to date (cf. also Kinney et al. (2003), p. 13). While there is extensive literature available regarding performance measurement and a wide, public debate is being conducted (cf. also the debate e.g. in controlling with Gleich (1997), Gleich/Brokemper (1998) and Mosiek (2002)), internal audit has been leading a shadowy existence so far in this respect.

The continuing scientific development of internal audit – not only on this subject – has appeared in a critical light so far. At this point, the question arises of whether business disciplines – particularly internal audit – are sustainable without a wide scientific basis and therefore without theoretical bases and methods. Extensive, practice-oriented publications ("from practice for practice"), audit guidelines and a comprehensive debate regarding standards dominate the foundation of internal audit. These debates are useful and necessary, but should not be the only, central seeds for the further development of internal audit.

The "internal audit" business discipline should expand its scientific foundation and the development of forward-looking business approaches more intensively, in order to keep up with the developments in other business areas and the emerging practical requirements.

The services, which internal audit undoubtedly performs, can be managed and communicated even more intensively on the basis of sound business measures. Then, it becomes clear that internal audit is not uncoupled from the company's business targets, but rather, can make a crucial contribution to these also being achieved.

Literature

Berry, L. L. and Parasuraman, A. (1999), Dienstleistungsmarketing fängt beim Mitarbeiter an, in: Bruhn, M. (Hrsg., 1999), Internes Marketing: Integration der Kunden- und Mitarbeiterperspektive, 2nd Edition, Wiesbaden 1999.

Blackmore, J., Foster, M. and Badenhorst, K. (2004), Internal Audit Benchmarking Survey, Ernst & Young South Africa, April 2004.

Breyer, M. (1999), Qualitätsmanagement von Beratungsdienstleistungen, Wiesbaden 1999.

Brown, M. A. (1997), Kennzahlen: harte und weiche Faktoren erkennen, messen und bewerten, Munich and Vienna 1997.

Buderath, H. M., Herzig, A., Köhler, A.G. und Pedell, B. (2010), Wertbeitrag der Internen Revision – Ansätze zur Messung, Steuerung und Kommunikation, Stuttgart 2010.

Buderath, H. und Langer, A. (2007), Eine kritische Perspektive zur wertorientierten Steuerung von Unternehmensbereichen am Beispiel der Internen Revision, in: Controlling, 19th Vol. 2007, No. 3. p. 129–135.

Deloitte & Touche (2008), Internal Audit – ERS Meeting, Stuttgart 2008 (internal presentation).

Deutsches Institut für Interne Revision e.V. (2002), IIR Revisionsstandard No. 3: Qualitätsmanagement in der Internen Revision, Frankfurt 2002.

Deutsches Institut für Interne Revision e.V. (2005), Die Interne Revision, Berlin 2005.

Deutsches Institut für Interne Revision e.V. (2007), Quality Assessment, 2nd Edition, Frankfurt a. M. 2007.

Frigo, M. L. (2002), The Institute of Internal Auditor, A Balanced Scorecard Framework for Internal Auditing Departments, Altamonte Springs 2002.

Gleich, R. (1997), Performance Measurement im Controlling, in: Gleich, R. und Seidenschwarz, W. (Hrsg., 1997), Die Kunst des Controlling, Munich 1997.

Gleich, R. (2001), Das System des Performance Measurement: Theoretisches Grundkonzept, Entwicklungs- und Anwendungsstand, Munich 2001.

Gleich, R. und Brokemper, A. (1998), Kunden- und Marktorientierung im Controllerbereich schaffen – 7 Schritte zur kontinuierlichen Leistungsplanung und -steuerung, in: Controller Magazin, 23. Jg., 1998, p. 148–156.

Hofmann, C. (2001), Anreizorientierte Controllingsysteme – Budgetierungs-, Ziel- und Verrechnungspreissysteme, Stuttgart 2001.

Hofmann, C. und Daugert, J. (2004), Bereichs- und Unternehmensbezogene Performancemaße zur Koordination und Steuerung von Bereichsleitern – Eine agency-theoretische Analyse, in: Scherm, E. and Pietsch, G. (Hrsg., 2004): Controlling – Theorien und Konzeptionen, Munich 2004.

Hölscher, L. und Rosenthal, J. (2007), Leistungsmessung der Internen Revision, Working Paper No. 86, Frankfurt 2007.

Horváth, P. (2008), Controlling, 11th Edition, Munich 2008.

Ittner, D. C., Larcker, D. F. und Meyer, M. W. (2003), Subjectivity and the Weighting of Performance Measures: Evidence from a Balanced Scorecard, in: Accounting Review, 78. Vol., 2003, 3, p. 725–758.

Jahn, J . (2007), Revision ist auch Knastprophylaxe, Frankfurter Allgemeine Zeitung, 13.10.2007, Nr. 238 / page C5.

Kaplan, R. P. und Norton, D. P. (1996), The balanced scorecard: translating strategy into action, Boston 1996.

Kinney et al. (2003), Global Internal Audit – the new reality, Deloitte Touche Tohmatsu 2003.

Klingebiel, N. (Hrsg., 2001), Performance measurement & balanced scorecard, Munich 2001.

Langer, A. (2007), Strategiekonforme Anreizsysteme für Führungskräfte teilautonomer Organisationseinheiten in der industriellen Produktion, Munich 2007.

Langer, A. und Munhoz, p. (2005), Qualitätssicherung und -steuerung für das Controlling bei der DaimlerChrylser do Brasil Ltda., in: Controlling, 17th Vol., 2005, p. 663–669.

Langer, A. und Pedell, B. (2010), Messung des Wertbeitrags der Internen Revision und dessen Integration in ein Performance Measurement-Konzept, in: Wertbeitrag der Internen Revision – Ansätze zur Messung, Steuerung und Kommunikation, ed. by Buderath, H. M., Herzig, A., Köhler, A.G. und Pedell, B., Stuttgart 2010, p. 45-105.

Likiermann, A. (2006), Measure for Measure, in: Internal Auditing & Business Risk, No. 1, 2006, p. 20–24.

Mosiek, T. (2002), Interne Kundenorientierung des Controllings, Frankfurt a. M., Berlin et al. 2002.

Schweitzer, M. (2001), Planung und Steuerung, in: Bea, F. X., Dichtl, E. and Schweitzer, M. (Hrsg.), Allgemeine Betriebswirtschaftslehre, 8. Auflage, Stuttgart 2001, p. 21.

The Institute of Internal Auditors (2007), QA CAE Annual Survey – Global Results, Altamonte Springs 2007.

The Institute of Internal Auditors (2007a), Standards for the Professional Practice of Internal Auditing, Altamonte Springs 2007.

Volkmann, M. (2007), Delphi-Methode, http://imihome.imi.uni-karlsruhe.de/ndelphi_methode_b.html, As of: June 2007.

Ziegenfuss, D. E. (2000), Measuring Performance, in: Internal Auditor, 57th Vol., 2000, H. 2, p. 36–41.

Zwingmann, L. (2006), Erwartungen an die Wertsteigerungsbeiträge der Internen Revision aus Sicht eines Geschäftsführers, IIR Annual Congress 2006 (Presentation).

Internal Auditor – Generalist or Specialist

By Dr. Heinrich Schmelter[73]

The work of internal audit is subject to a constant change and further development process. With this, the speed of change is increasing and makes increasingly higher demands on the internal auditor. This article deals with the provocative thesis, "Internal Auditor – Generalist or Specialist".

1   Careers based on Status and Specialism

Fig. 1 shows the potential career paths of auditors in an industrial company. After university studies (generally Graduate in Business Administration or Graduate in Engineering), young auditors can advance from audit assistant, to auditor and senior auditor. Other career options are chief auditor and ultimately, internal audit manager.

The auditors working in industrial companies can accordingly be roughly classified into 5 career status levels:

– audit assistant
– auditor
– senior auditor
– chief auditor or decentralised audit manager
– internal audit manager

For some of the internal auditors, the aim could be to move to the specialist departments – e.g. after 5 years at the earliest. Conversely, internal audit departments sometimes also recruit employees, who have previously already worked in a specialist department. The aim of the personnel strategy could be a mixture of 50 % permanent audit employees – with long-term experience – and 50 % employees moving into or out of the department, with only a temporary audit activity[74].

---

[73] Dr. Heinrich Schmelter has been working in management functions for 30 years (audit, controlling and IT), in the automobile industry.
[74] Cf. Zwingmann (2007), p. 52.

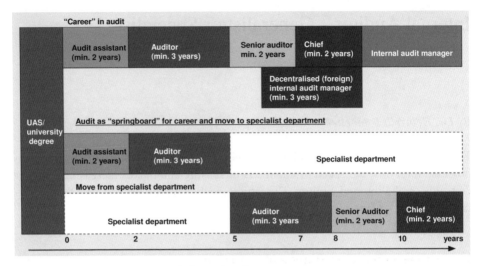

Figure 1: Professional career paths in internal audit

The prevailing organisation of large internal audit departments in industrial companies shown in Fig. 2, is usually structured functionally, in a process-oriented manner, according to the most important business processes. The internal auditors are each assigned to chief auditors. The managers of large group audit departments also filled the position of internal audit managers of decentralised internal audit departments of domestic and foreign subsidiaries, above a "dotted line" (as technical management)[75].

Some of the chief auditors frequently have a "business audit" main department assigned to them; the auditors working here are primarily regarded as business-oriented auditors. The second main department, "technical audit" can have the technically-oriented logistical and construction audit assigned to it. IT audit usually has employees working in it with very good IT knowledge (mainly computer scientists), in purchasing/logistics audit, there are mainly graduate engineers and in construction audit, there are usually civil engineers. The "Special Investigations" chief auditor may possibly report directly to the internal audit manager. The employees working there mainly have a business degree, but they also have specialist methodological knowledge, as special investigators.

The auditors working in large audit departments in industry can usually be roughly classified into 4 specialist professional groups:

---

[75] Cf. Wagner (2005), p. 143.

1. business auditor
2. technical auditor
3. IT auditor
4. special investigator

2 Twelve General and Specific Requirements for Internal Auditors

The requirements for internal auditors can be split into 5 general and 7 specialist categories (cf. Fig. 3–5):

General requirements:
1. Ability to work in a team
2. Flexibility
3. Leadership skills
4. Company knowledge
5. Process knowledge

Specialist requirements:
1. Professional ethos
2. Internal audit methodology
3. Internal control and risk management knowledge
4. Internal audit experience
5. Financial knowledge
6. Technology knowledge
7. IT knowledge

2.1 General Ability to Work in a Team

The well-developed ability to work in a team is an essential, general characteristic for any internal auditor. Internal auditors work in changing teams with different colleagues and are in contact with constantly new employees and managers in the audited areas for each audit. The work in a changing audit team can only take place meaningfully with employees who are very capable of working in a team, who deal with new audit tasks very flexibly together, with constantly changing colleagues. Also in contact with the audited areas, friendly – but naturally also consistent/authoritative/active – auditors are required, who encounter the audited areas in a collegial and outgoing manner[76].

In the role also currently aimed at, of being an advisor, collegial, persuasive powers also count, rather than "superior assertion using borrowed management powers".

---

[76] Cf. Zwingmann (2007), p. 46.

125

With critical audit findings, the auditor should convince the specialist departments – in a team-oriented manner – about the necessary process improvements and not only enforce recommendations "by means of reporting to the highest hierarchy levels".

2.2 General Flexibility

High flexibility is also an essential basic requirement for auditors. Auditors work on approx. 3 to 6 different, large audits per year. The audits are frequently not very standardised and each requires very quick familiarisation with constantly new subjects. For technically competent, well-founded audits, the necessary specialist skills need to be gained quickly, with effective and efficient audit approaches based on these. If necessary, the auditors must be able to review and assess even the most difficult factual issues very quickly.

Beyond the technical familiarisation skills, flexibility is also required regarding willingness to travel and adaptable personal conduct. Experienced auditors must be able to move flexibly and confidently, also abroad[77] and work well together with audited persons at all hierarchy levels. Even an auditor at the clerical level must be able to soundly communicate his/her critical findings and recommendations to a management board member.

2.3 General Leadership Skills

Leadership skills and experiences are, of course, very highly dependent on the status of the internal audit employee. For internal audit managers, particularly in multi-level audit divisions of large companies, well-developed leadership characteristics are essential. Audit department managers and chief auditors, as well as auditors, must be able to deal confidently with management staff at all levels, right up to the management board.[78] With decentralised audits, e.g. in a foreign company or factory, it is also expected that every auditor can report adequately to the local top managers (e.g. factory manager) regarding the audit results.

2.4 General (and Specific) Company Knowledge

Auditors should be as familiar as possible with "their" company. After repeatedly new audit assignments, experienced auditors – more than any other professional group in the company – become familiar with all specialist departments. In awareness of the different specifics of the specialist departments, audits can be conducted significantly more quickly, efficiently and effectively, without needing to newly

---

[77] Cf. Federschmidt (2006), p. 238.
[78] Cf. Zwingmann (2007), p. 46.

acquire all of the basic company knowledge in advance. (In this regard, internal auditors should have a significant knowledge advantage over external auditors.)

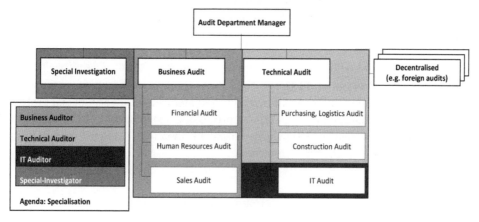

Figure 2: Example organisation of large audit departments

Chief auditors are also expected to have profound detailed knowledge about their specialist field for specific audit areas (e.g. treasury), so that they can always communicate competently with their specialist department partners.

In contrast, the internal audit manager should have knowledge about the company that is as extensive as possible. Because he/she must be responsible for the audit reports for all departments, he/she should have a good understanding of all core technical divisions, over and above the self-evident, detailed knowledge regarding the finance department.

2.5   General (and Specific) Process Knowledge

In parallel with specialist department knowledge, as far as possible, auditors should at least be familiar with all core processes of "their" company. Efficient and effective performance audits with cross-departmental process recommendations are only possible with knowledge about the basic process relationships.[79]

In addition to the internal process specifications, chief auditors who are responsible for specific audit areas (e.g. treasury) should also be aware of the best practice approaches for their specialist process area, so that they not only examine compliance with internal provisions, but can also competently advise their specialist department partners in a process-oriented manner.

---

[79]   Cf. Binner (2005), p. 50.

The internal audit manager must be familiar with all of the company's core processes. Only in this way, can he/she understand and implement cross-departmental process improvement recommendations. This wide-ranging, basic process knowledge is also necessary for the internal audit manager's function as the "top" risk manager of a company.

2.6 Specific Professional Ethos

Internal auditors are (similar to external auditors) members of a very special professional group with particularly high ethical professional standards[80], [81], [82]. The most important of the professional standards below are therefore explicitly anchored in CIA examinations[83]:

- Righteousness
- Objectivity
- Confidentiality

Someone can only be an auditor, who fully embodies there professional standards in his/her personal performance. Any doubt regarding integrity discredits the auditor/the respective internal audit department and destroys the value of any audit result, in the individual case.

2.7 Specific Internal Control and Risk Management Knowledge

Internal control and risk management include specific specialist knowledge, which can only – and almost exclusively – be found in the internal audit department within companies. In accordance with the prime internal audit function of supporting the management board in its monitoring function, the audit department must primarily ensure the functionality of internal control and ensure sufficient risk management[84]. In order to actually be able to fulfil this internal audit and advisory function, the auditors must have the relevant specialist knowledge and professional experience[85]. Because neither internal control, nor risk management are common (university) education subjects, these specific professional requirements essentially need to be learned internally in internal audit, from practical experience.

---

[80] Cf. Deutsches Institut für Interne Revision, Code of Professional Ethics, 2002.

[81] Cf. Bantleon (2008), p. 106.

[82] Cf. Tesch (2007), p. 144.

[83] Cf. The International Institute of Internal Auditors, Certified Internal Auditor.

[84] Cf. Zwingmann (2007), p. 47.

[85] Cf. Gröflin (2004), p. 798.

2.8 Specific Internal Audit Methodology

The internal audit manager and his/her chief auditors are also the guardians of the internal audit work methodology. Through personal instruction and internal (manual) specifications, they must guide all auditors to carry out efficient and effective work. With increasing experience, each auditor must become familiar with the internal tools of audit and implement them consistently. The work methods particularly include standardised approaches with risk analysis, audit planning, preparation, implementation, post-processing (with archiving of working documents), reporting and follow-up. Depending on the audit area, the auditors must also be familiar with specific audit steps (e.g. with construction projects) and/or have a command of specific (quick) analyses (e.g. with special investigations).

2.9 Specific Internal Audit Experience

The internal audit experience is the collective product of many years of work in internal audit. Beyond internal audit methodology, internal control and risk management specialist knowledge, it also relates to company and process knowledge that is as extensive as possible. While an internal audit beginner particularly requires more extensive instructions by his/her chief auditor, a senior must also be able to handle the most difficult audits independently, thereby formulating best practice process improvement recommendations.

It is expected from chief auditors and from internal audit managers that, as internal audit professionals, they are able to cover their audit area/the entire company confidently, as well-informed auditors, as well as competent advisors.

2.10 Specific Financial Knowledge

Financial knowledge is an absolute must for any auditor, because, regardless of the audit area, knowledge regarding the financial process is also necessary for virtually any audit. This means that basic financial knowledge also always needs to be expected from technical auditors. Finance-oriented auditors, who primarily work in the areas of treasury, accounting and controlling, or also in human resources, should have completed degree studies as graduates in business administration and preferably also have practical finance experience. Internal auditors in the banking sector should also have vocational training in banking.

2.11 Specific Technical Knowledge

Particularly in large industrial companies, some of the auditors also need well-founded technical knowledge on the basis of degree studies in engineering. In order to encounter the audited areas in production, development, purchasing and logistics, an auditor must understand the "language" of these departments and also be able to familiarise themselves with technical details, if necessary. In large companies with large internal audit departments, a specialist construction audit department is also recommended, which should preferably be staffed with experienced civil engineers.

Because virtually all processes in industrial companies have a technical character, all of the internal auditors should generally have a good basic understanding of technology and the specific products of the respective company. Experience has shown that without technical basic knowledge and product knowledge, business-oriented audits, e.g. in purchasing, logistics or sales, are also initially sub-optimal.

2.12 Specific IT Knowledge

As virtually all of the processes in the companies can now only be handled with IT support and personal computers are a matter of course as personal tools, an auditor without good IT knowledge is no longer conceivable. The required full-audit of large data volumes can only take place with a good knowledge of specific audit software (e.g. ACL). With the calculation, reporting and poss. presentation of audit results, efficient work is only possible with practical experience in common office software tools (e.g. EXCEL, WORD and POWERPOINT). IT knowledge beyond this, also regarding mainframe computer software, is particularly essential for IT auditors, because they can otherwise not communicate professionally with the audited IT areas.

3 Professional Status Requirements

Fig. 3 shows the requirement categories, differentiated by professional status. It relates to finance-oriented auditors with a senior auditor as a comparison basis (see section with wide, grey border).

A good level of specific finance knowledge is primarily expected from a finance-oriented senior auditor. So that finance-oriented audits can be conducted efficiently, adequate IT knowledge must also be available. In accordance with his/her senior experience, a senior auditor should also work perfectly regarding audit methodology and be a competent advisor for internal control issues. After several years in a company, he/she should have general company and process knowledge and have specific, detailed knowledge of the finance area. Professional ethos and the ability to work in a team must be very well-trained. As a senior auditor, high flexibility must also exist for diverse assignment options.

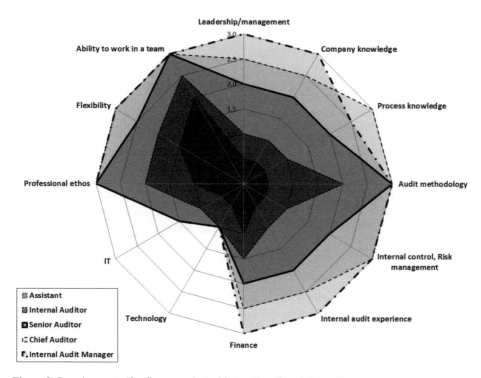

Figure 3: Requirements (for finance-oriented internal auditors) depending on status

For chief auditors in the finance area, beyond having good theoretical, specialist finance knowledge, practical experience is expected from them in finance audit areas and processes. Regarding internal control, he/she must be the best specialist advisor in the company, together with the internal audit manager. In accordance with his/her leadership function, the chief auditor should have good leadership skills to manage 1-5 auditors assigned to him/her.

The internal audit manager, with overall responsibility, must naturally have the highest leadership skills. Also regarding professional ethos, methodology, flexibility, ability to work in a team and knowledge about the company, he/she should be "the best" in the internal audit team. In terms of process knowledge, a wide overview tends to apply more to him/her, than the necessary detailed knowledge about specific audit areas required by chief auditors. However, in accordance with the expectations for internal audit, a very good knowledge of the finance area continues to be primarily expected from the internal audit manager of an industrial company. Of course, the performance of a senior auditor can initially only be expected from auditors and audit assistants to a limited extent. However, in order to be assignable to the finance area, good theoretical finance knowledge should always form a basis.

Essential basic requirements for "beginners" in internal audit are also always high flexibility, conducting oneself with integrity and the ability to work in a team.

4   Requirements According to Professional Specialist Field

Fig. 4 shows the 12 requirement categories, differentiated according to professional specialist field. In this case, a finance-oriented senior auditor again serves as a basis for comparison (see section with wide, grey border).

The illustration shows identical general professional requirements for all professional specialist fields, which have already been described above for the finance-oriented senior auditor. With the specialist internal control knowledge, similarly high requirements also exist for finance-oriented, technically-oriented and IT-oriented senior auditors, of course, always with the expectation of having the necessary specific internal control experience in the finance, technology or IT environment.

In accordance with the professional specialist field, a distinction is only made between the requirements regarding the specialist necessary knowledge and experience. A finance auditor, and even more, a bank auditor, must have particularly well-developed specialist finance knowledge. In industrial companies, at least, a minimum of basic technical knowledge is also expected from finance-oriented auditors.

Auditors in the technical audit area should have training as a graduate engineer for their audit field. However, in order to also be able to audit all of the accounting-related technical aspects (e.g. price changes), each technical auditor must also have basic finance knowledge.

5   Dependencies of the requirements on company size and sector

The orientation of the internal audit team, and therefore also the requirements for internal auditors, have a high dependency on the respective company size and sector.

In large companies with more than 50,000 employees and more than 20 internal audit staff, a significantly stronger specialisation by the auditors is necessary and possible, than in a medium-sized company with only a few internal audit employees. In internationally active, global corporate groups with more than 100,000 employees, the central internal audit divisions, with their branch offices, usually have more than 100 internal auditors. With this magnitude, it is necessary and possible to assign IT auditors and internal audit specialists for special investigations, in addition to business-oriented and technically-oriented auditors. Even within business audit, an additional specialisation is possible according to treasury, accounting and human resources audit. In technical audit, highly specialised civil engineers can also be assigned to audit construction projects. Within the context of joint audits, specialists in central internal audit can support the smaller, decentralised internal audit units with difficult specialist audits (e.g. in treasury).

Also in companies from a size of approx. 10,000 employees with internal audit departments comprised of more than 5 auditors, a differentiation generally already takes place according to business and technical auditors, as well as a specialist IT auditor.

In even smaller companies/internal audit departments, the few auditors are inevitably more generalists, because they personally need to cover all audit fields; however, generally, these auditor work more on an accounting-oriented basis, in order to primarily ensure compliance/truth and fairness requirements.

The company sector also has a basic influence on the internal audit orientation and the requirements for the respective auditors. In industrial companies, technical audit is usually also necessary, because most of the divisions, particularly those in production and development with many employees, can only be audited with a technical background. In contrast the audits in trading and banking are primarily aimed toward commercial truth and fairness requirements. Particularly with financial service providers, additional state audit requirements (particularly by the financial regulatory authority, BaFin) need to be fulfilled, which can usually only be fulfilled with specifically trained bank auditors. Auditors working in the field of government authorities need to be even more specifically oriented and trained. Auditors with highly specialised audit assignments particularly work in tax audit, financial supervisory audit and trade control audit.

6   The "Ideal" Internal Auditor

In summary, the "ideal" internal auditor is a multifaceted, flexible employee, who personally also combines contradictory professional requirements, in some cases (see Fig. 5 for finance oriented senior auditor in comparison to a beginner – minimum requirements):

–   He/she has graduated with honours, either as a Graduate in Business Administration or a Graduate in Engineering. Also as a technical auditor, he/she has business (particularly truth and fairness) basic financial knowledge. Conversely, a finance-oriented auditor in an industrial company has basic technical knowledge, in order to e.g. also handle audits in mixed audit areas, such as logistics or purchasing. Therefore, degree studies as an industrial engineer would be ideal for an "ideal" auditor, who could be assigned diversely.

– Detailed, conscientious audit work forms the professional basis for any internal auditor. The "ideal" auditor always works highly efficiently, i.e. very quickly and deadline-oriented, in spite of the essential accuracy requirements.

– Although he/she generally acts very independently and judgementally as an integral "team fighter" in an audit sub-area, the internal auditor is able to cooperate well in very team-oriented manner in a constantly changing audit team with different colleagues.

– Although it is required that he/she is an independent, objective, "incorruptible" auditor, he/she always confronts the employees in all hierarchies in a very collegial manner and convinces, rather than acting "superior".

– In doing so, he simultaneously acts as an expert (detail) auditor, as well as a convincing process advisor[86], [87]. Particularly regarding internal control and risk management[88], he/she is always regarded as a competent advisor in the company.

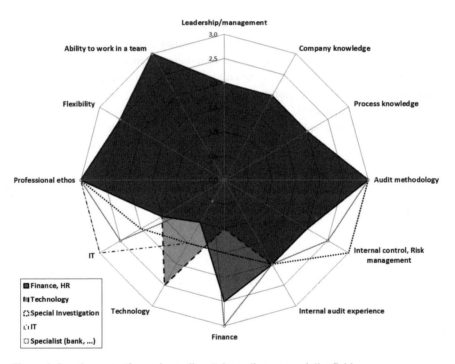

Figure 4: Requirements (for senior auditors) depending on specialist field

---

[86]   Cf. Kundinger (2006), p. 198.

[87]   Cf. Binner (2005), p. 50.

[88]   Cf. Reinecke (2000), p. 194.

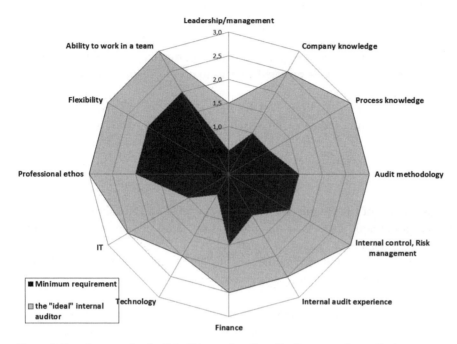

Figure 5: Requirements for the "ideal" internal auditor (for finance senior auditor)

− On the internal audit clerk level, the "ideal" auditor is also able to confidently communicate his/her audit findings as any time, if required, even at the management board level.
− This particularly also include very good oral and written expression, which culminates in brief and concise audit reports for the highest company levels.
− For the follow-up, the "ideal" auditor consistently and skilfully advocates his/her recommendations, without spoon-feeding the audited areas too much in detail.
− The very experienced "ideal" auditor has an overview of the entire company with all of its core processes, from diverse audits. If required, he/she is very flexible and can also familiarise himself/herself with every detail very quickly.
− In order to work as efficiently and effectively as possible, he/she uses all of the modern audit methods, particularly the currently available IT support options. With the aid of IT, he/she conducts 100 % full audits, as far as possible, in order to achieve preferably far-reaching audit results within a short time.
− Without forgetting the self-evidence truth and fairness and internal control requirements, the "ideal" auditor develops very effective audit approaches, which also enable potential performance improvement in a process-oriented manner.

The – partially contradictory – requirements for the ideal senior auditor are so high, that such an "ideal auditor" can usually only be "kept" at the management levels of internal audit. In fact, during the course of the envisaged job rotation, the best employees are frequently poached by the specialist department, so that internal audit – as a potential talent foundry" – repeatedly needs to develop good new blood.

Even if the "ideal" auditor is a rarity on the clerical level, the internal audit manager needs to primarily find candidates, when selecting personnel, who particularly have a great ability to work in a team and flexibility, as well as undoubted professional ethos, as a minimum requirement, in addition to a promising university degree.

7   Summary of the Requirements as a Generalist and Specialist

As the reader certainly expects as this point, at the latest, the answer to the initial question is, of course, not "generalist or specialist", but rather, "generalist and specialist". Each internal auditor, regardless of his/her status or specialist field, must combine general and specific professional requirements.

With increasing responsibility, the generalist in the internal auditor becomes more and more important. In addition to excellent specialist audit experience, the internal audit manager ultimately needs to have generalist experience and a generalist view. Because internal audit covers the entire company with all of its processes and areas, very good overall company knowledge is essential for the diverse audit reports. In order to satisfy the expectations of the management board, as the internal audit client, all auditors, but particularly the internal audit manager, need to have a general management board view.

This means that every internal auditor – also as a beginner – must basically be able to fulfil a generalist requirement, in spite of having a function that is initially specialised. Even if not every auditor can advance to a chief auditor or internal audit manager, particularly with process-oriented audits, every auditor should have an overall company view and pursue a management-board-oriented assessment with the weighting of his/her audit findings.

However, the generalist requirements can only be fulfilled on the basis of specific knowledge and experience of internal audit working methodology. Each auditor and chief auditor is naturally initially a specialist in the processes and truth and fairness requirements in his/her audit field; at the same time, it is expected from internal audit and each auditor that they can appear as the most competent specialist in the company for internal control and risk management. This audit and advisory activity is ultimately also based on the specific professional ethos regarding personal integrity and objectivity.

From everything mentioned above, it becomes clear that an efficient and effective, modern internal auditor must satisfy diverse, high professional requirements, which exceed the requirements of many other professional groups. In view of this, the function of modern internal audit is a major professional challenge with very good career prospects.

Literature

Binner, H.; Rieckmann, P.: Geschäftsprozesse – analysieren, optimieren und modellieren, in: ZIR 5/2005, p. 50.

Bantleon, U.; Unmuth, A.: Das internationale Regelwerk der Beruflichen Praxis des Institute of Internal Auditors (IIA), in: ZIR 3/ 2008, p. 106.

Deutsches Institut für Interne Revision, Code of Professional Ethics, Internet site (www.diir.de), as of 2009.

Deutsches Institut für Interne Revision, CIA Examinations, Internet site (www.diir.de), as of 2009.

Federschmidt, C.; Langer, A.: Interkulturelle Aspekte bei Revisionen im Ausland, in: ZIR 6/2006, p. 238.

Freidank, C.-C.; Lachnit, L.; Tesch, J.: Vahlens Großes Auditing Lexikon, Munich, 2007.

Gröflin, M.: Zur Zukunft der Internen Revision, in: Der Schweizer Treuhänder, 10.2004.

Institute of Internal Auditors (IIA), Certified Internal Auditor (CIA), Internet site (www.theiia.org/certification/certified-internal auditor/), as of 2009.

Institute of Internal Auditors, Certified Internal Auditor, Internet site (www.theiia.org/certification/certified-internal-auditor/), as of 2009.

Kundinger, P.: Die Interne Revision als Change Agent, in: ZIR 5/2006. p. 198.

Reinecke, B.: Risiko-Aspekte in der Arbeit der Internen Revision, in: ZIR 5/2000. p. 194.

Tesch, C.; Lammert, J.: Berufsethik des Wirtschaftsprüfers, in:

Freidank, C.-C.; Lachnit, L.; Tesch, J.: Vahlens Großes Auditing Lexikon, Munichen, 2007, p. 144.

Wagner, H. J.: Erfahrungen bei der Erstprüfung von Beteiligungsgesellschaften, in: ZIR 4/2005, p. 142.

Zwingmann, L.: Erwartungen an die Wertsteigerungsbeiträge der Internen Revision, in: ZIR 2/2007, p. 47.

Audit Marketing

By Dr. Hannes Schuh[89]

The esteem in which a company holds its Internal Audit department can be increased by targeted marketing measures. It is worth considering audit marketing beyond the numerous, mainly process-oriented measures available in the literature and applying the logic of marketing.

1   Audit Marketing as a Part of General Marketing

As part of the general marketing concept, which refers to the company as a whole[90] and comprises the penetration of the overall organization with a focus on addressees or stakeholder groups, i.e. customers, shareholders, the company's own departments[91], audit marketing focuses on Internal Audit Unit's exchange relationships in the overall organization.

Accordingly, the key issue for audit marketing is:

> With which marketing tools can the acceptance and impact of Internal Audit Units be improved in the overall organization?

On the one hand audit marketing focuses on the position of Internal Audit Unit in the company, while on the other it is also associated with the marketing-oriented focus of the overall organization based on the claim that it adds value. This means that the message at the heart of its marketing activities is not "The Internal Audit Unit is a (very) good department in the company", but that "The Internal Audit Unit actively adds value to the company with high-quality measures!"

The audit of the efficiency and to a certain extent the effectiveness of the company's marketing is also a part of the audit universe, but this will not be discussed further here.

---

[89]   Dr. Hannes Schuh is an audit manager in an Austrian ministry and a board member of the IIA Austria. The article originates largely from his book "Interne Revisionen im öffentlichen Sektor" (Internal audits in the public sector).

[90]   Kotler (1980) defines marketing as follows: "Marketing is getting the right goods and services to the right people at the right place at the right time at the right price with the right communication and promotion."

[91]   Cf. Scheuch F., "Einführung Marketing" (Introduction to marketing), p. 3

2   Examples of the Current Status of Audit Marketing

According to the IIA Austria, audit marketing includes[92]:

- the internal selling of newly implemented Internal Audit Units,
- informing managers of the main work, benefit and advantage of Internal Audit Unit (at management events)
- transparent information on Internal Audit Unit (in the intranet)
- informing employees of the audited organizational unit (at the introductory meeting)
- obtaining feedback (after the interviews, for example as part of the final meeting – in writing or verbally)
- revealing best-practice solutions (as part of audits or advisory assignments)
- presenting Internal Audit Unit as a competent contact and/or problem solver beyond specific audits.

In terms of an audit employee concept, the German Institute for Internal Auditing views this as follows[93]:

In addition to relevant publications and attendance at internal and external events, it is particularly important to present possible development paths, the education concept, the systematic preparation for management tasks transparently and where possible to support these with examples.

It also makes sense to show Internal Audit Unit's contribution to the company's success using specific examples.

A few of these support measures for employee recruitment are mentioned below:

- lectures about Audit at internal events / seminars
- articles about Audit in company magazines
- presentation about Audit in the intranet
- publications on audit issues in professional journals
- lectures at conferences/congresses or in universities.

Numerous possible measures are listed in the German literature, but there is hardly a systematic approach to audit marketing.

---

[92]   IIA Austria, "Interne Revision – Gestaltung und Organisation in der Praxis" (Internal audit – structure and organization in practice), p. 19 f.

[93]   German Institute for Internal Auditing, "Konzept zur Gewinnung und Qualifizierung von Mitarbeitern für die Interne Revision" (Concept for the recruitment and training of employees for internal audit), p. 5 f.

3   Marketing Approach for Internal Audit

By roughly applying the principles of marketing, the following picture emerges:

3.1   Market Form

The products of Internal Audit are audit, advice, and, to some extent a special form of advice, information.

An analysis of the structure of supply and demand by competitive situation (monopoly, oligopoly and polypoly) produces the following scenarios:

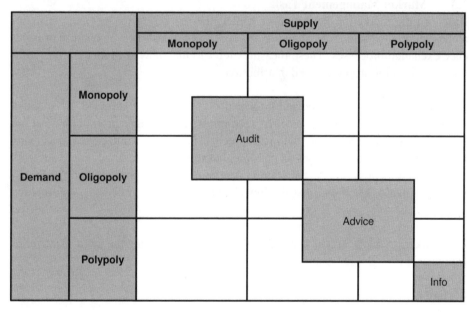

Figure 1: Market form for IA products

Apart from when the audit is considered in the narrowest sense (the audit is performed by IA on behalf of top management), the audit is in a supply-oligopoly position because the Court of Auditors to some extent other external auditors and in any event though internal auditors perform process-integrated audit controls. On the demand side often top managers (oligopoly) initiate the audit.

With advice there are a few or many suppliers and a few or many customers.

In any event the mere provision of information is located in the area of supply and demand polypoly.

3.2   Exchange Relationship

With regard to the forming of exchange relationships concerned with marketing decisions, a distinction has to be made with regard to the audit activities:

–   Audit, advice and information are Internal Audit services for the whole company which should ultimately serve to support the company in achieving its goals and ensure the organization is fit for the requirements of the future.
–   The exchange relationship exists between the high-quality services of Internal Audit and a change by the organization.

3.3   Market Management Task

Based on the marketing definition of Kotler, the marketing management tasks include the targeted selection, planning and control of measures which cause or influence exchange processes. These measures refer to the areas of product, price, communication, sales promotion and distribution.

The products are audit, advice and information. The price is expressed in the added value created by the realization of IIA recommendations. Sales promotion must not be viewed quantitatively here, but qualitatively. The goal is not to carry out as many simple audits and consultations as possible, but to solve difficult audit and advisory tasks as well as possible. Distribution is determined by the product type (audit, advice, information) and the distribution channel (reporting processes, information media, etc.).

The marketing management task can therefore be defined for the audit manager as follows:

–   targeted selection,
–   planning, performance and control of audits,
–   provision of advice and information by Internal Audit,

which allow the company to better achieve its goals and to be better prepared for the demands of the future.

3.4.   Environment Analysis

Groups

The relationship of the customers to the products of the Internal Audit Unit can be outlined as follows:

	Audit	Advice	Information
Internal customers			
Top management level	Customer and report addressee		Overall view of the organization
(Audit Board)	(Customer and report addressee)		Overall view of the organization
Managers	Persons audited and/or responsible for imple-mentation	Use IA's expertise	View of organization and own department
Project managers	Persons audited and/or responsible for imple-mentation	Use IA's expertise	View of organization and own department
Employees	Persons audited		View of own depart-ment
Crime auditors	Addressee of relevant audit findings for own audits	Use IA's expertise (e.g. preventive measures)	View crime-relevant weak points in the organization
Auditors of the line organization	Use results in own audits	Use IA's expertise (audit system)	View of organization and own department
External customers			
Audit office	Use results in own audits		
Other external auditors (e.g. ac-counting company)	(Use results in own audits)		
Audit community		Use IA's expertise (audit system)	View of audit system

Table 1: Audit customers

Customer Benefits

An initial rough assessment of the customer benefits of Internal Audit Unit by the scope and content of information reveals the following picture:

		Scope of information		
		Audit	**Advice**	**Information**
Content of information	**Individual issues**	Determination of the facts, evaluation, recommendation, agreement	Keynote presentations, workshops etc. in the core competences	
	Systems	Risk minimization, quality improvement based on risk-oriented audit plans	Improvement potential concerning risk management systems, internal control systems	condensed view of systems and their potential; audit system
	Overall organization	Value added to the organization with the implementation of the recommendation / agreement, contribution towards the organization being fit for the future	Improvement potential concerning corporate risk management, corporate governance	critical view of the overall situation and strategic need for change

Table 2: Customer benefits

In contrast to other functions in the organization, the following appears to be relevant:

– Internal Audit Unit acts independently.
– It knows the administrative culture precisely.
– It can address any issue and goes far beyond financial and regularity aspects.
– The selection of issues takes place on a risk-oriented basis and goes far beyond an annual plan towards a medium and long-term risk map.
– Its work is (mostly) confidential and is not published, unlike for example with Court of Auditors.
– Internal Audit Unit's technical knowledge covers the whole area of the audit universe.
– IA is oriented towards the strategy of management, adds value and contributes towards the organization being fit, etc.

Competition
Product categories:
Audit reports are in competition with quality assurance tools (e.g. self-assessment).

Product variants:
As well as the audit reports from Internal Audit Unit, there are also audit reports from external auditors and other internal auditors.

There is much greater competition for advice and information; please refer to the supply structure outlined above.

3.5   Marketing Tools
Finally the quality of Internal Audit Unit and the benefits for the overall organization have to be presented in coordinated campaigns throughout the year in a manner suitable for the product and target group. In particular contrast to its external competition, its independent position and embedding in the corporate culture should be emphasized.

Such a marketing mix could look like this:

Internal Audit brand
– Corporate Design (independent, but in keeping with the CD of the company)
– Presentation[94] of IA at
  o   Information events for all employees ("tour", ca. every 3 years)
  o   Information via external Quality Assessments (ca. every 4 to 5 years)
  o   Change in the top management level
  o   Request for audit suggestions from managers (annual)
  o   Signing of the annual audit plan (annual)
  o   Annual report (annual)
  o   Start of audit (per audit case)
  o   Obtain feedback (per audit case), etc.
– Knowledge map about Internal Audit (intranet)
– Presentation of the knowledge and success of employees (company magazine, intranet)
  o   Degrees
  o   Certifications
  o   Roles in national and international associations
  o   Roles in international workgroups and projects
  o   National and international presentations

---

[94]   Massive differences in presentation depending on the addressee and purpose!

- o   Activities at universities, colleges, academies
- o   Career steps, etc.

Products
Audit
–   Audit Charter
–   Brochures on the audit process
–   Information at the initial meeting on audit goals and methods (verbal and hand-out)
–   Final audit report (preparatory documents, final meeting, draft report)
–   Final report with regard to
    - o   content, including (if necessary) introduction to the audit issue
    - o   presentation form
    - o   Communication path
–   Communication concerning quality assurance and impact
    - o   feedback on the specific audit
    - o   informal meetings between the audit manager and managers
    - o   follow-up

Advice outside of an audit includes:
–   lectures,
–   workshops,
–   advisory meetings,
–   reflections about concepts, etc.

in particular concerning
- o   quantitative and qualitative audit methods
- o   internal control systems
- o   risk management
- o   corporate governance
- o   fraud
- o   organizational change

The supply of advisory services is rather restricted due to the contradiction between audit and advice. The tools which are associated with the IA brand and which target managers are most likely to be effective.

In view of Internal Audit Unit's often rather small contribution to the comprehensive changes, IA's performance must in no way be singled out. The account will probably be restricted to the overall presentation, such as for example in the annual report.

With regard to **information**, among others the following marketing tools can be used

- Annual feedback to managers
- Presentations at management meetings
- Lectures
- Employee training, e.g. in internal academy
- Written expert opinions (as opposed to advice on own initiative)
- Communication of internal audit measures as a result of own quality assurance
- Best-practice example of Internal Audit Unit as a pioneer of modern working methods (teamwork, networking, long-distance solutions, etc.)

4   Summary

The application of generally recognized marketing logic to audit marketing results in a new, comprehensive approach to existing IA marketing measures in the literature and opens up new methods.

It seems important to be aware that, although IA offers only a few products, these are diverse, that these have to be positioned in a diverse market environment, and even the audit or audit report does not have a monopoly position.

The marketing management task is to select, plan an implement suitable measures and is to be performed by the audit manager.

May this article encourage management professionals and audit managers to tackle the issue together.

Literature

DIIR (employee concept)
    German Institute for Internal Auditing, "Konzept zur Gewinnung und Qualifizierung von Mitarbeitern für die Interne Revision" (Concept for the recruitment and training of employees for internal audit), Frankfurt am Main, 2002
IIRÖ (IA – structure and organization)
    IIA Austria, "Interne Revision – Gestaltung und Organisation in der Praxis" (Internal audit – structure and organization in practice), Linde Verlag, Vienna, 2008
Scheuch F. (Introduction to marketing)
    Lecture notes on "introduction to marketing", Vienna University of Economics and Business, 2007
Schuh H. (Internal audits in the public sector)
    "Interne Revisionen im öffentlichen Sektor – Organisatorische Ausrichtung für die Zukunft" (Internal audits in the public sector – organizational alignment for the future), Linde Verlag and Boorberg Verlag, 2010

List of Authors

Neil Baker is a journalist and writer. He is the editor of Internal Auditing, the IIA – UK and Ireland's magazine, and a director at Smith de Wint, which publishes European Internal Audit Briefing for the ECIIA.

Philipp Friebe, lic. oec. publ., is doctoral candidate at the institute for Accounting and Control at the University of Zurich, Switzerland and research assistant at the Institute of Accounting, Control and Auditing at the University of St. Gallen, Switzerland.

Adrián Garrido, CIA, has more than 20 years experience in Auditing, control, risk and finance at the banking industry. He has actively participated in several projects as Basel II, SOX, M&A and strategic plans. He is Certified Internal Auditor and won the "I Eduardo Hevia award of the Institute of Internal Auditors of Spain on innovation in internal auditing". Currently he is the Head of Internal Audit – South America Region at BBVA Group.

Prof. Dr. Fikret Hadžić is an associate professor at the School of Economics and Business in Sarajevo at the University of Sarajevo. He is also successfully engaged in business consulting in financing, banking and investment area. As a consultant he has worked on more than two hundred investment and consulting projects for local and overseas clients. He is the author of several professional and scientific papers presented and published at national and international symposia, congresses and conferences. He is the author of several books on banking, especially in the field of Islamic economics, banking and finance. He was manager of several projects, author and co-author of several studies as well as the experts team leader of the UNDP Project Early Warning System B&H in 2002, 2003, and 2004. He is a member of the Supervisory Board of the Development Bank of the Federation of Bosnia and Herzegovina as well as a member of the Organizing Committee of the Symposium and a Program Committee of the Association of Internal Auditors in B&H recognized as the Institute of Internal Auditors in B&H at IIA Global.

Andreas Herzig is a Partner at Deloitte responsible for the Competency Area Business Risk Solutions in Germany. He actively works on an improvement of methods to measure value added through Internal Audit by combining Risk Management, Controlling and Quality Assessment approaches. He has published several articles on that topic and is Co-Publisher / Co-Author of the book 'Wertbeitrag der Internen Revision' / Value Added through Internal Audit (published autumn 2010).

Shqiponja Isufi, lic. oec. publ., is doctoral candidate at the Institute for Accounting and Control at the University of Zurich, Switzerland and research assistant at the Institute of Accounting, Control and Auditing at the University of St. Gallen, Switzerland.

Dr. Andreas Langer is a Manager at Deloitte in Germany. He is responsible for the Deloitte-Service "Performance Driven Internal Audit". He has published several articles in the areas of Internal Audit and Performance Management and is Co-Author of the book 'Wertbeitrag der Internen Revision' / Value Added through Internal Audit (published autumn 2010).

Thomas Lohre, MBA, CISA, CISM is currently member of the ISO-27001-project team at DATEV eG, an IT-Service Provider in Nuremberg. Prior to his current position he worked for a period of 7 years as an IT-Auditor at DATEV eG specialized in auditing risk management, software develpment processess and protection of information assets. He writes articles with the focus on IT-Compliance, Corporate Governance and IT-Auditing.

Sergey Martynov, (CISA, CIA, CFE) is President of the Russia Chapter of the Association of Certified Fraud Examiners. He is also a chairman of the audit committee and a board member of three energy companies: Kuzbassenergo OJSC (TGK-12), Yeniseiskaya TGK OJSC (TGK-13) and Far Eastern Energy OJSC. In August 2005 he was appointed Chief Audit Executive in the Siberian Coal Energy Company. Earlier headed internal audit and internal control departments of large oil and telecommunication companies and also led projects on internal audit and internal control systems creation for the largest enterprises of fuel and energy complex of Russia.

Daniel Nelson, (CPA, CIA), is the Assistant Director of the Office of Internal Audit and Inspection at the International Monetary Fund (IMF), in Washington DC. He is responsible for the management of all aspects of internal audit activities at the Fund. He is an alternate member of the Fund's Advisory Committee on Risk Management, and works as Senior Personnel Manager for the Office of the Managing Director. Daniel Nelson is also a member of the audit committee of the United Nations Children's Fund (UNICEF). Prior to the IMF, Daniel Nelson was Director of Internal Audit at the UN World Food Programme (WFP). He has a Laurea in Economia e Commercio from the Libera Universita' degli Studi Sociali (LUISS), Rome.

Inta Ozolina (ACCA, CIA) is an internal audit manager at telecoms operator. She has previously worked with the consulting department PricewaterhouseCoopers (specialised in internal audit and risk management related services to clients) and internal auditor in an energy company. She has also delivered training courses on risk management and internal audit. Inta's background is B.Sc. in Economics and Business Administration (Stockholm School of Economics in Riga), M.A. in International Economic Relations (University of Latvia) and B.A. in Education (University in Latvia).

Prof. Dr. Burkhard Pedell, is holding the Chair of Management Accounting and Control at the University of Stuttgart. He is member of the Scientific Committee of the German Institute of Internal Auditing. Burkhard's research fields include Value Based Management, Risk Management, Performance Measurement and Incentive Systems, Cost Management, Internal Audit and Compliance as well as Rate Regulation. He is Co-Publisher and Co-Author of the book 'Wertbeitrag der Internen Revision (Value Added through Internal Audit)', published autumn 2010.

Flemming Ruud, Ph.D., CPA (Norw.), is Professor of Business Administration, in particular Internal Control / Internal Audit at the University of St. Gallen, Switzerland. In addition, he is Adjunct Professor of Internal and External Auditing at the Norwegian School of Management, Oslo, Norway, and at the University of Toronto, Canada. Prior to this, he was Professor of Accountancy and Internal Auditing at the University of Zurich, Switzerland. Since 1997, he is a member of the board of the IIA Switzerland (Institute of Internal Auditing Switzerland), and recently, he took over the lead of the ECIIA Task Force for Academic Relations. He also functions as advisor to European academic institutions, auditing firms, governments and businesses, promoting the development of corporate governance, financial and operational auditing. His research areas encompass internal control, internal auditing, and financial issues of corporate governance.

Dr. Heinrich Schmelter, is retired and actually works as an author for audit issues. Previously he was manager for audit, controlling and information-technology in the automotive industry. He has always been a particular specialist in the IT support of audit.

Daniela Schmitz, lic. oec. publ., is doctoral candidate and research assistant at the Institute of Accounting and Control at the University of Zurich, Switzerland.

Hannes Schuh, is Chief Audit Executive of the Austrian Ministry of Finance and Vice President of the Austrian Institute of Internal Auditors. Additionally he is engaged as a member of the Board of Auditors of the European Patent Office and as a guest lecturer at a university of applied studies, at the Federal Academy of Public Administration and at the Federal Tax and Customs Academy. Furthermore he is recognised as co-editor (e.g. Austrian Tax Journal), author and international expert.

He holds a doctoral degree in laws (University Vienna) and an MBA in public auditing (University of Busniess Administration and Economics Vienna).

Amir Softić, is a Board Member of ASA Group BH in charge of the risk management on the Group level. Parallel to his ordinary job, Amir Softic is engaged as a lector in the Banking Academy of School of Economics and Business in Sarajevo. Prior to this, he was Head of Department of Risk Management Department of HVB Bank Bosnia and Hercegovina. In that period he has set up a very efficient credit process with integrated decision making tools in the retail segment (private individuals and SME). One of the most important results Amir Softic achieved in that period is linked to decrease of NPL ratio by 11 %.